Brownies, Bars, & Biscotti!

Brownies, Bars, & Biscotti!
by Terri Henry

Specialty Cookbook Series Edited by Andrea Chesman

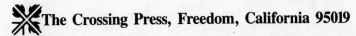The Crossing Press, Freedom, California 95019

This collection of recipes is dedicated to my mom, Bernice Henry, whose patience and guidance in the kitchen while I was learning to bake will forever be appreciated.

Copyright © 1989 by Terri Henry
Cover illustration and design by Betsy Bayley
Text illustration and design by Betsy Bayley
Printed in the U.S.A.

The Crossing Press Specialty Cookbook Series

Library of Congress Cataloging-in-Publication Data

Henry, Terri, 1960–
    Brownies, bars & biscotti / Terri Henry.
       p. cm. — (Specialty cookbook series)
    Includes index.
    ISBN 0-89594-365-4
    1. Biscuits. 2. Brownies (Cookery) 3. Cookies. I. Title.
II. Series.
TX770.B55H46 1989
641.8'654—dc20

89–9961
CIP

Contents

1. Brownies 7

2. Fruit and Nut Bars 51

3. Biscotti 91

Index 121

I
Brownies

What satisfies a chocolate craving better than a rich, sweet brownie? The staple of children's picnics and school bake sales for years, brownies have grown up. Not only do they taste just as good with a steaming cup of coffee as they do with a tall glass of ice cold milk, but they can be made with an infinite variety of flavors, including raspberry, coconut, and peppermint. Until you've tasted a Hawaiian Brownie, a Cherry Oat Brownie, or a Coconut Fudge Dream, you haven't lived.

The recipes contained in this section are straightforward and easy to follow—a few even start with store-bought mixes so that even the beginning baker can have guaranteed results.

The real tricks to assuring success with brownie making are to measure each ingredient carefully, to avoid burning the chocolate as you melt it, and to take care not to overbake your brownies.

Chocolate should be melted over very low heat because it tends to burn easily. You may wish to use a double boiler for this process.

When melting baking chocolate alone or with butter or margarine, break the chocolate into small pieces before heating to insure faster melting and to reduce the chance of scorching.

To melt chocolate in a microwave, break the chocolate into small pieces and put into a microwave-safe bowl. Cover with plastic wrap and melt according to the manufacturer's directions. The timing will depend on the quantity of chocolate and the size of the bowl.

Unless otherwise indicated, brownie batters can be combined using an electric mixer or hand mixer, or by beating by hand with a large spoon. Obviously, if you are pressed for time, an electric mixer is fastest. After the wet and dry ingredients are mixed, any nuts, chocolate chips, butterscotch bits, etc. should be folded in by hand, taking care that they are evenly distributed throughout the batter.

Brownies can also be mixed in a food processor. Using a metal blade, coarsely chop the *unmelted* baking chocolate, turning the processor on and off several times. Add the sugar and continue processing until the chocolate is as fine as the sugar. Add the softened butter or margarine, processing until the mixture is creamed. Then add the egg, salt, extracts, and other flavorings until the mixture is fluffy. Combine the dry ingredients in another bowl and add to the wet ingredients, turning the processor on and off several times and taking care not to overprocess. Then fold in the nuts, chocolate chips, butterscotch bits, etc. by hand.

Overbaking brownies is the most common mistake even experienced bakers make. Because oven temperatures vary, you can't rely exclusively on the timing given in the recipes. When fudge brownies are done, the top will look dry and shiny, but the center of the brownie will still look very moist and underdone. Cake brownies (these will contain baking powder or baking soda) can be tested for doneness by inserting a toothpick into the center of the pan. When the toothpick is removed clean, the brownies are done.

After removing brownies from the oven, place the pan on a wire cooling rack. Allow the brownies to cool completely, or you will have difficulty cutting them cleanly and removing them from the pan in one piece.

Brownies can be stored in the pan in which they were baked, covered, at room temperature for several days. For longer storage, refrigerate for up to 1 week. Fudgy brownies freeze best when individually wrapped in plastic wrap or aluminum foil. I do not recommend freezing cake-style brownies as they tend to dry out. Frozen brownies will keep for several months (if they last that long). To defrost, remove the brownie from its wrapper and allow to stand at room temperature for 15 minutes.

A Few Words About Chocolate

In this collection of recipes, I have used several different types of chocolate to add variety and different flavors to the recipes.

Unsweetened Baking Chocolate. Unsweetened baking chocolate has a rich, bitter flavor that makes the perfect base for a brownie, and I use this form of chocolate more frequently than any other. It traditionally comes in individually wrapped 1-ounce squares and is usually melted before it is used in a recipe. (If you are mixing in a food processor, you can skip the melting stage and just finely chop it.) Take care when melting squares of chocolate to avoid scorching them—use low heat or melt in a microwave. Recently, premelted packets of baking chocolate have appeared on the market. While the premelted chocolate can be used as a convenient substitute for the squares, I prefer not to use it. Premelted chocolate is more expensive than chocolate squares. Moreover, the chocolate generally contains palm oil, which is high in cholesterol.

Semi-Sweet Chocolate. This chocolate has a rich, dark flavor, which makes it excellent for eating out of hand or for using in baking. It is made of unsweetened chocolate that has been blended with sugar, cocoa butter, and flavorings. Semi-sweet chocolate can be purchased in bar form or in bags of chocolate chips, morsels, or bits. A 6-ounce bag of chips contains 1 cup of pieces and a 12-ounce bag contains 2 cups.

Milk Chocolate. Made of chocolate liquor blended with cocoa butter, milk or cream, sugar, and flavors, milk chocolate is rarely used in baking because it does not impart a very strong flavor.

Unsweetened Cocoa Powder. This is a form of chocolate in which a proportion of the cocoa butter has been removed. The remaining liquid hardens and is then pulverized, with the result being a pure, acidic powder that has good, if bitter, flavor. It must be combined with sugar for baking and drinking. When combining cocoa powder with melted butter or margarine, make sure all the lumps are removed before you blend in the other ingredients.

White Chocolate. White chocolate isn't made of chocolate at all. It contains 30 percent cocoa butter (which gives it the chocolaty flavor), 30 percent milk solids, and 30 percent sugar (which makes it sweeter than real chocolate). It also contains vanilla for flavoring. Do not confuse white chocolate with white confectionery coating, which substitutes vegetable oil for cocoa butter; read the package carefully.

White chocolate can be difficult to melt and tends to become grainy if overheated, so melt carefully over very low heat.

Any time a recipe calls for unsweetened baking chocolate, you can substitute unsweetened cocoa powder and extra butter or margarine. For every ounce of unsweetened baking chocolate called for, substitute 3 level tablespoons of unsweetened cocoa powder combined with 1 tablespoon melted butter or margarine. Make sure all the lumps are removed before you add this mixture to the other ingredients.

Classic Fudge Brownies

If you are looking for a classic, fudgy brownie, rich in chocolate flavor and packed with walnuts, this is the recipe to try.

3 ounces unsweetened baking chocolate
1 cup white sugar
1 cup firmly packed brown sugar
⅓ cup light corn syrup
½ cup butter or margarine, softened
4 eggs
1¼ cups all-purpose flour
1 cup chopped walnuts

Preheat the oven to 350° F. Grease a 9-inch by 13-inch pan.

Melt the chocolate in the top of a double boiler and set aside.

Mix together the sugars, corn syrup, and butter or margarine, but do not cream. Add the eggs, one at a time. Slowly pour in the chocolate, mixing well. Add the flour, beating until smooth. Fold in the walnuts. Spread the batter in the prepared pan and bake for 25 to 30 minutes. Place the pan on a wire rack and allow to cool completely before cutting into squares.

Yield: 24 brownies

Frosted Fudge Brownies

Brownies

4 ounces unsweetened baking chocolate
1 cup butter or margarine
4 eggs
2 cups sugar
2 teaspoons vanilla extract
1 cup all-purpose flour
¾ cup chopped walnuts

Fudge Frosting

4 ounces unsweetened baking chocolate
2 cups sugar
2 eggs, beaten
¼ cup light cream
¼ cup butter or margarine
2 teaspoons vanilla extract

Yield: 24 brownies

Preheat the oven to 350° F. Grease a 9-inch by 13-inch pan.

Melt the chocolate and butter or margarine over low heat. Set aside to cool slightly.

Beat together the eggs and sugar until frothy. Add the vanilla. Slowly pour in the chocolate mixture, mixing well. Add the flour, beating until smooth. Fold in the walnuts. Spread in the prepared pan and bake for 25 to 30 minutes. Place the pan on a wire rack and allow to cool completely before frosting.

To make the frosting, melt the chocolate over low heat in a medium-size saucepan. Add sugar, eggs, cream, butter or margarine, and vanilla, mixing well. Increase heat and bring to a boil, stirring constantly. Remove from the heat and let cool slightly. Spread over the cooled brownies and allow to set before cutting into squares.

Double Chocolate Brownies

With the addition of chocolate chips to an already dense brownie, these may be the fudgiest brownies you'll ever taste.

4 ounces unsweetened baking chocolate
1 cup butter or margarine
4 eggs
2¼ cups sugar
2 teaspoons vanilla extract
1 cup all-purpose flour
1 cup semi-sweet chocolate chips

Preheat the oven to 350° F. Grease a 9-inch by 13-inch pan.

Melt the chocolate and butter or margarine over low heat and set aside to cool slightly.

Beat the eggs and sugar until frothy. Add the vanilla. Slowly pour in the chocolate mixture, mixing well. Add the flour and beat until smooth. Fold in the chocolate chips. Spread the batter in the prepared pan and bake for 25 to 30 minutes. Place the pan on a wire rack and allow to cool completely before cutting into squares.

Double Chocolate Fruit Brownies

Substitute 2 to 3 tablespoons cherry or strawberry extract for the vanilla.

Yield: 24 brownies

Crème de Cacao Brownies

Subtly flavored with chocolate liqueur, these go very well with an after-dinner cup of coffee.

2 ounces unsweetened baking chocolate
½ cup butter or margarine
2 eggs
1 cup sugar
¼ cup crème de cacao
⅔ cup all-purpose flour
¾ cup chopped pecans

Preheat the oven to 350° F. Grease an 8-inch square pan.

Melt the chocolate and butter or margarine over low heat. Set aside to cool slightly.

Beat together the eggs and sugar until frothy. Slowly add the chocolate mixture and crème de cacao. Add the flour and beat until smooth. Fold in the pecans. Spread in the prepared pan and bake for 30 minutes. Place the pan on a wire rack and allow to cool completely before cutting into squares.

Grand Marnier Brownies

Substitute ⅓ cup Grand Marnier or any other orange liqueur for the crème de cacao.

Yield: 16 brownies

Raspberry Brownies

Sweet, fruity raspberry preserves are swirled through the dark, rich, melt-in-your-mouth brownies.

3 ounces unsweetened baking chocolate
⅓ cup butter or margarine
2 eggs
1¼ cups sugar
1 teaspoon vanilla extract
¾ cup all-purpose flour
¼ cup high-quality raspberry preserves

Preheat the oven to 350° F. Grease an 8-inch square pan.

Melt the chocolate and butter or margarine over low heat. Set aside.

Beat together the eggs and sugar until frothy. Add the vanilla. Slowly add the chocolate mixture, mixing well. Add the flour, beating until smooth. Spread the batter in the prepared pan.

Drop spoonfuls of raspberry preserves on the batter. Zigzag a knife or spatula through the batter to marble in the preserves. Bake for 25 minutes. Place the pan on a wire rack and allow to cool completely before cutting into squares.

Yield: 16 brownies

Fruited Brownies.

Substitute any high-quality fruit preserves (blackberry, strawberry, peach, apricot, etc.) for the raspberry preserves.

Brownie Fruit Bars

The chewiness of raisins and dates make a nice contrast to the crunch of pecans and butter brickle bits.

2 ounces unsweetened baking chocolate
½ cup butter or margarine
2 eggs
1 cup sugar
1 teaspoon vanilla extract
⅔ cup all-purpose flour
½ cup raisins
½ cup chopped dates
1 cup chopped pecans
1 cup butter brickle baking bits

Preheat the oven to 350° F. Grease an 8-inch square pan.

Melt the chocolate and butter or margarine over low heat. Set aside to cool slightly.

Beat together the eggs and sugar until frothy. Slowly add the chocolate mixture and vanilla, mixing well. Add the flour and beat until smooth. Fold in the raisins, dates, and pecans. Spread in the prepared pan and bake for 25 minutes. Remove from the oven. Sprinkle the butter brickle baking bits over the brownies. Return to the oven and bake for 5 minutes more. Place the pan on a wire rack and cool completely before cutting into squares.

Quick Brownie Fruit Bars

Prepare a 15½-ounce package of brownie mix

Yield: 16 brownies

as the package directs for fudge-type brownies. Fold in the raisins, dates, and pecans as above. Bake for 30 minutes and proceed with the recipe as above.

Honey Pecan Brownies

Pure, sweet honey gives these brownies their chewy goodness.

Brownies

½ cup butter or margarine
½ cup sugar
⅓ cup honey
1 teaspoon vanilla extract
2 eggs
½ cup all-purpose flour
⅓ cup unsweetened cocoa powder
⅔ cup chopped pecans

Yield: 16 brownies

Honey Icing

3 tablespoons butter or margarine, softened
3 tablespoons unsweetened cocoa powder
½ teaspoon vanilla extract
1 cup confectioners' sugar
1 tablespoon milk
1 tablespoon honey

Preheat the oven to 350° F. Grease an 8-inch square pan.

In a large bowl, beat together the butter or margarine and sugar until fluffy. Add the honey and vanilla. Add the eggs, mixing well.

Combine the flour and cocoa powder and add to the egg mixture, beating until smooth. Fold in the pecans. Spread the batter in the prepared pan and bake for 25 to 30 minutes.

Place the pan on a wire rack and allow to cool completely before frosting.

To make the frosting, cream the butter or margarine in a small mixing bowl until light and fluffy. Add the cocoa powder, vanilla, confectioners' sugar, milk, and honey. Beat until smooth. Spread over the cooled brownies and allow to set before cutting into squares.

Raisin Fudge Brownies

Chewy raisins and crunchy walnuts make these brownies irresistible.

2 ounces unsweetened baking chocolate
½ cup butter or margarine
2 eggs
1 cup sugar
1 teaspoon vanilla extract
½ cup all-purpose flour
1 cup golden raisins
½ cup chopped walnuts

Preheat the oven to 350° F. Grease an 8-inch square pan.

Melt the chocolate and butter or margarine over very low heat. Remove from the heat and allow to cool slightly.

Beat together the eggs and sugar until frothy. Add the vanilla. Slowly add the chocolate mixture, then the flour, beating until smooth. Gently fold in the raisins and walnuts. Spread the batter in the prepared pan and bake for 25 to 30 minutes. Place the pan on a wire rack and allow to cool completely before cutting into squares.

Yield: 16 brownies

Milk Chocolate Brownies

The chocolate flavor in these is not as intense as the flavor that results from using semi-sweet or unsweetened chocolate, but the brownies are quite tasty just the same. Any milk chocolate candy bar can be used in this recipe.

4 ounces milk chocolate candy
½ cup butter or margarine
2 eggs
¾ cup sugar
1 teaspoon vanilla extract
¾ cup all-purpose flour
½ cup chopped walnuts or pecans
  (optional)

Preheat the oven to 350° F. Grease an 8-inch square pan.

Melt the chocolate and butter or margarine over low heat. Set aside to cool slightly.

Beat together the eggs and sugar until frothy. Add the vanilla. Add the flour, beating until smooth. Fold in the nuts, if desired. Spread the batter in the prepared pan and bake for 25 minutes. Place the pan on a wire rack and allow to cool completely before cutting into squares.

Yield: 16 brownies

Chewy White Chocolate Brownies

These exceptionally dense brownies have the added crunch of butter brickle. Although made with white chocolate, the brownies bake up a light golden brown.

1⅓ cups white chocolate baking chips
6 tablespoons butter or margarine
2 eggs
½ cup sugar
1½ teaspoons vanilla extract
½ cup all-purpose flour
⅓ cup butter brickle baking bits

Preheat the oven to 350° F. Grease an 8-inch square pan.

Melt 1 cup of the white chocolate chips and the butter or margarine over low heat. Set aside to cool slightly.

Beat together the eggs and sugar until frothy. Add the vanilla. Slowly mix in the chocolate mixture. Gradually add the flour and beat until smooth. Spread the batter in the prepared pan. Sprinkle with the remaining ⅓ cup white chocolate chips and butter brickle bits. Bake for 30 to 35 minutes. Place the pan on a wire rack and allow to cool completely before cutting into squares.

Yield: 16 brownies

Marbled Brownies

⅓ cup butter or margarine, softened
1 cup sugar
2 eggs
1 teaspoon vanilla extract
½ cup all-purpose flour
¼ cup semi-sweet chocolate chips

Preheat the oven to 350° F. Grease an 8-inch square pan.

Beat together the butter or margarine and sugar until fluffy. Beat in the eggs and vanilla. Add the flour, beating until smooth. Pour half of the batter into the prepared pan.

Melt the chocolate chips over very low heat. Add the melted chocolate to the batter remaining in the bowl, mixing well.

Spread the chocolate batter over the white batter in the pan. Zigzag a knife or spatula through the layered batters to marble the chocolate into the white. Bake for 25 minutes. Place the pan on a wire rack and allow to cool completely before cutting into squares.

Yield: 16 brownies

Layered Peppermint Brownies

Here's the perfect brownies for the Christmas holiday season, especially if you add a few drops of red or green food coloring to the second layer.

Layer 1

2 ounces unsweetened baking chocolate
½ cup butter or margarine
2 eggs
1 cup sugar
½ cup all-purpose flour
½ cup chopped walnuts or pecans

Layer 2

1½ cups confectioners' sugar
3 tablespoons butter or margarine, softened
2 tablespoons milk
1 teaspoon peppermint extract
A few drops red or green food coloring (optional)

Layer 3

½ cup semi-sweet chocolate chips
1 tablespoon butter or margarine

Yield: 16 brownies

Preheat the oven to 350° F. Grease an 8-inch square pan.

Melt the chocolate and butter or margarine over low heat for the first layer. Remove from the heat and set aside to cool slightly.

Beat together the eggs and sugar until frothy. Add the chocolate mixture, mixing well. Add the flour, beating until smooth. Fold in the nuts. Spread the batter in the prepared pan and bake for 20 minutes. Remove from the oven. Place the pan on a wire rack and allow to cool completely.

To make the second layer, cream together the confectioners' sugar and butter or margarine. Blend in the milk, peppermint extract, and food coloring, if desired. Spread on top of the cooled first layer. Refrigerate until chilled.

To make the top layer, melt the chocolate chips and butter or margarine over low heat. Cool slightly and drizzle over the peppermint layer. Chill thoroughly, then cut into squares.

Macaroon Brownies

Here is a dense, fudgy brownie with a sweet coconut topping.

3 ounces unsweetened baking chocolate
½ cup butter or margarine
3 eggs
¾ cup sugar
1½ teaspoons vanilla extract
½ cup all-purpose flour
½ cup sweetened condensed milk
2¼ cups sweetened shredded coconut

Preheat the oven to 350° F. Grease an 8-inch square pan.

Melt the chocolate and butter or margarine in a saucepan over low heat. Remove from the heat and set aside to cool slightly.

Beat together the eggs and sugar until frothy. Add the chocolate mixture and vanilla, mixing well. Add the flour and beat until smooth. Spread the batter in the prepared pan.

Combine the condensed milk and coconut. Spoon the mixture over the batter. Bake for 30 to 35 minutes. Place the pan on a wire rack and allow to cool completely before cutting into squares.

Yield: 16 brownies

Layered Oat Brownies

The best of two worlds—oatmeal cookie on the bottom with fudge brownie on the top.

Brownies

¾ cup butter or margarine, softened
1½ cups white sugar
2 eggs
1 teaspoon vanilla extract
¾ cup flour
½ cup unsweetened cocoa powder

Crust

2½ cups rolled oats (regular or quick)
¾ cup all-purpose flour
¾ cup firmly packed brown sugar
½ teaspoon baking soda
¾ cup butter or margarine, softened

Yield: 24 brownies

Preheat the oven to 350° F. Grease a 9-inch by 13-inch pan.

To make the brownies, beat together the butter and sugar until fluffy. Add the eggs and vanilla, mixing well.

Combine the flour and cocoa. Add to the egg mixture, beating until smooth. Set aside.

Stir together the oats, flour, brown sugar, and baking soda. Work in the butter or margarine until the mixture is crumbly. Reserve ¾ cup of the oat mixture and press the remaining mixture in the bottom of the prepared pan. Bake for 10 minutes. Remove from the oven and let cool slightly.

Spread the prepared brownie batter over the baked crust. Sprinkle with the reserved oat mixture. Bake for 25 to 30 minutes. Place the pan on a wire rack and allow to cool completely before cutting into squares.

Classic Cake Brownies

From an old family recipe, Classic Cake Brownies have a light cake-like texture. If a fancier brownie is desired, frost with your favorite frosting.

½ cup butter or margarine
1½ cups firmly packed brown sugar
1 egg
½ cup milk
1½ cups all-purpose flour
½ teaspoon baking soda
3 tablespoons unsweetened cocoa powder
½ cup hot water
¼ cup chopped walnuts or pecans

Preheat the oven to 350° F. Grease an 8-inch square pan.

Cream together the butter or margarine and brown sugar until fluffy. Gradually add the egg and milk, mixing well.

Combine the flour, baking soda, and cocoa powder. Add to the egg mixture alternately with the hot water, beating until smooth. Fold in the nuts. Spread the batter in the prepared pan and bake for 25 to 30 minutes. Place the pan on a wire rack and allow to cool completely before frosting or cutting into squares.

Yield: 16 brownies

Chocolate Syrup Brownies

Chocolate syrup makes a moist, dense brownie.

½ cup butter or margarine, softened
1 cup sugar
2 eggs
1 teaspoon vanilla extract
1¼ cups all-purpose flour
¼ teaspoon baking soda
¾ cup chocolate syrup (canned or bottled)
½ cup chopped walnuts or pecans

Preheat the oven to 350° F. Grease a 9-inch by 13-inch pan.

Beat together the butter or margarine and sugar until fluffy. Add the eggs and vanilla.

In a separate bowl, combine the flour and baking soda; add to the egg mixture alternately with the chocolate syrup. Beat until smooth. Fold in the nuts. Spread the batter in the prepared pan and bake for 40 to 45 minutes. Place the pan on a wire rack and allow to cool completely before cutting into squares.

Yield: 24 brownies

Buttermilk Brownies

Brownies

2 cups all-purpose flour
2 cups sugar
1 cup butter or margarine
¼ cup unsweetened cocoa powder
1 cup cold water
½ cup buttermilk
1 teaspoon vanilla extract
1 teaspoon baking soda
2 eggs

Cocoa-Nut Icing

½ cup butter or margarine
¼ cup unsweetened cocoa powder
5 tablespoons milk
1 teaspoon vanilla extract
¾ cup chopped walnuts or pecans
1 (16-ounce) box confectioners' sugar

Yield: 32 brownies

Preheat the oven to 400° F. Grease an 11-inch by 17-inch jelly roll pan.

Combine the flour and sugar in a large bowl. Set aside.

In a medium-size saucepan, combine the butter or margarine, cocoa powder, and water and bring to a rolling boil. Remove from the heat and pour over the flour and sugar mixture. Mix well. While the mixture is still warm, add the buttermilk, vanilla, baking soda, and egg, beating until smooth. Spread the batter in the prepared pan and bake for 20 minutes.

Five minutes before the baking time is up, prepare the icing. In a medium-size saucepan, combine the butter or margarine, cocoa powder, and milk. Bring to a boil. Remove from

the heat. Add the vanilla, nuts, and confectioners' sugar. Beat until smooth.

Place the brownie pan on a wire rack and
allow the brownies to cool for 5 minutes, then
spread with the icing. Cool completely before
cutting into squares.

Applesauce Brownies

The addition of unsweetened applesauce to these cake-like brownies makes them especially moist and adds a subtle, tangy taste.

3 ounces unsweetened baking chocolate
1 cup butter or margarine
4 eggs
2 cups sugar
1 cup unsweetened applesauce
2 teaspoons vanilla extract
2 cups all-purpose flour
1 teaspoon baking powder
½ teaspoon baking soda
1 cup chopped walnuts or pecans
Sifted confectioners' sugar

Preheat the oven to 350° F. Grease a 9-inch by 13-inch pan.

Melt the chocolate and butter or margarine over low heat. Set aside to cool slightly.

Beat together the eggs and sugar until frothy. Add the applesauce and vanilla, mixing well. Gradually add the chocolate mixture, mixing well.

Combine the flour, baking powder, and baking soda. Add to egg mixture, beating until the batter is very smooth. Fold in the nuts. Spread the batter in the prepared pan and bake for 30 minutes. Place the pan on a wire rack and allow to cool completely. Sprinkle the top of the brownies with sifted confectioners' sugar. Cut into squares.

Yield: 24 brownies

Rolo Brownies

Everyone I know loves Rolo candies—those bite-size caramels that are covered in milk chocolate. In this recipe, melted Rolo candies provide a chewy caramel topping for the brownies. You can find Rolos wherever candies are sold.

1 cup sugar
½ cup vegetable oil
2 eggs
1 teaspoon vanilla extract
⅔ cup all-purpose flour
½ cup unsweetened cocoa powder
½ teaspoon baking powder
1 (9-ounce) package individually wrapped Rolo candy pieces (about 40 pieces)
1 tablespoon milk
½ cup chopped walnuts or pecans

Yield: 16 brownies

Preheat the oven to 350° F. Grease an 8-inch square pan.

Beat together the sugar and oil until frothy. Add the eggs and vanilla.

Combine the flour, cocoa powder, and baking powder. Add to the egg mixture, beating until smooth. Spread the batter in the prepared pan and bake for 25 to 30 minutes.

In a saucepan, combine the Rolo candy pieces with the milk and melt over very low heat, stirring constantly. Spread over the warm brownies. Sprinkle with the nuts. Place the pan on a wire rack and allow to cool completely before cutting into squares.

Cherry Oat Brownies

Brownies

½ cup semi-sweet chocolate chips
⅔ cup butter or margarine
2 eggs
1 cup sugar
1 teaspoon vanilla extract
1¼ cups all-purpose flour
¾ cup rolled oats (regular or quick)
1 teaspoon baking powder
1 (16-ounce) jar maraschino cherries, drained and chopped
½ cup chopped walnuts or pecans

Chocolate Glaze

½ cup semi-sweet chocolate chips
1 tablespoon butter or margarine

Yield: 24 brownies

Preheat the oven to 350° F. Grease a 9-inch by 13-inch pan.

Melt the ½ cup semi-sweet chocolate chips and ⅔ cup butter or margarine over low heat. Set aside to cool slightly.

Beat together the eggs and sugar until frothy. Add the vanilla, then the chocolate mixture.

Combine the flour, oats, and baking powder. Gradually add to the egg mixture, mixing well. Gently fold in the cherries and nuts. Spread the batter in the pan and bake for 25 minutes. Place the pan on a wire rack and cool completely while making the chocolate glaze.

Melt the remaining semi-sweet chocolate chips and butter or margarine over low heat, stirring until the mixture is smooth. Drizzle over the cooled brownies. Cut into squares.

Coconut Fudge Dreams

Instead of candy on Valentines Day, give the object of your affection a batch of Coconut Fudge Dreams—the brownies to win someone's heart!

2 ounces unsweetened baking chocolate
2 cups semi-sweet chocolate chips
2 tablespoons butter or margarine
2 eggs
¾ cup sugar
2 tablespoons instant coffee powder
1 teaspoon vanilla extract
¼ cup all-purpose flour
¼ teaspoon baking powder
½ cup chopped pecans
½ cup sweetened shredded coconut

Preheat the oven to 350° F. Grease an 8-inch square pan.

Melt the unsweetened chocolate, 1 cup of the chocolate chips, and the butter or margarine over low heat. Set aside to cool slightly.

In medium-size bowl, beat together the eggs and sugar until frothy. Add the coffee powder, vanilla, and chocolate mixture. Mix well.

Combine the flour and baking powder and add to the egg mixture, beating until smooth. Fold in the remaining 1 cup chocolate chips, the pecans, and coconut. Spread the batter in the prepared pan and bake for 20 to 25 minutes. Place the pan on a wire rack and allow to cool completely before cutting into squares.

Yield: 16 brownies

Hawaiian Brownies

I call these Hawaiian Brownies because I add macadamia nuts, pineapple, and cinnamon to the batter. These two-layer, cake-like brownies have a rich, exotic flavor.

Brownies

3 ounces unsweetened baking chocolate
1 cup butter or margarine
2 cups sugar
4 eggs
1 teaspoon vanilla extract
1½ cups all-purpose flour
½ teaspoon baking powder
¼ teaspoon cinnamon
1 (15½-ounce) can unsweetened crushed
   pineapple, drained very well
½ cup chopped macadamia nuts

Yield: 24 brownies

Vanilla Icing (optional)

1 cup confectioners' sugar
1 tablespoon butter or margarine, softened
2 tablespoons milk
½ teaspoon vanilla extract

Preheat the oven to 350° F. Grease a 9-inch by 13-inch pan.

Melt the chocolate over very low heat. Set aside.

Beat together the butter or margarine and sugar until fluffy. Add the eggs and vanilla, mixing well.

Combine the flour, baking powder, and cinnamon. Add to the egg mixture, beating until smooth.

Measure out 1½ cups of the batter and stir

in the pineapple. Set aside. Mix the melted chocolate into the remaining batter. Fold in the nuts. Spread the chocolate batter in the prepared pan. Spread the pineapple batter evenly over the top. Bake for 40 to 45 minutes. Place the pan on a wire rack and allow to cool completely while you make the frosting, if desired.

Combine all the frosting ingredients in a small bowl. Beat until smooth. Spread over the cooled brownies. Allow the frosting to set before cutting the brownies into squares.

Cream Cheese Brownies

Swirled through and through with creamy, smooth cream cheese, Cream Cheese Brownies are a rich-tasting cross between a brownie and cheesecake.

4 ounces semi-sweet baking chocolate
5 tablespoons butter or margarine, softened
1 (3-ounce) package cream cheese, softened
1 cup sugar
3 eggs
1 tablespoon plus ½ cup all-purpose flour
1½ teaspoons vanilla extract
½ teaspoon baking powder
½ cup chopped walnuts

Yield: 16 brownies

Preheat the oven to 350° F. Grease an 8-inch square pan.

Melt the chocolate and 3 tablespoons of the butter or margarine over low heat. Set aside.

Beat the remaining 2 tablespoons butter or margarine with the cream cheese. Gradually add ¼ cup of the sugar. Beat until fluffy. Beat in 1 of the eggs, 1 tablespoon flour, and ½ teaspoon of the vanilla. Set aside.

Beat the remaining 2 eggs and ¾ cup sugar until frothy. Slowly add the chocolate mixture, mixing well. Add the vanilla.

Combine the remaining ½ cup flour and the baking powder. Add to the chocolate batter, beating until smooth. Fold in the walnuts.

Spread half of the chocolate batter in the prepared pan. Top with the cream cheese mix.

Spoon the remaining chocolate batter over the top. Zigzag a knife or spatula through the batter to marble in the chocolate. Bake for 30 minutes. Place the pan on a wire rack and allow to cool completely before cutting into squares.

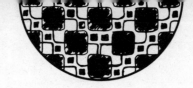

Almond White Chocolate Brownies

A hint of almond extract adds depth to the bland sweetness of white chocolate.

4 ounces white chocolate
⅔ cup butter or margarine
3 eggs
1 cup sugar
½ teaspoon almond extract
1 cup all-purpose flour
½ cup chopped almonds

Preheat the oven to 325° F. Grease a 9-inch by 13-inch pan.

Melt the chocolate and butter or margarine over low heat. Set aside to cool slightly.

Beat together the eggs and sugar until frothy. Add the almond extract. Slowly add the chocolate mixture, mixing well. Add the flour and beat until smooth. Fold in the almonds. Spread the batter in the prepared pan and bake for 25 minutes, or until slightly browned on top. Place the pan on a wire rack and allow to cool completely before cutting into squares.

Yield: 24 brownies

Chocolate Crunch Brownies

This recipe makes a three-layer treat consisting of a cake-like brownie bottom, a gooey marshmallow center, and a crispy peanutty-chocolate topping.

½ cup butter or margarine
¾ cup sugar
2 eggs
1 teaspoon vanilla extract
¾ cup all-purpose flour
¼ teaspoon baking powder
2 tablespoons unsweetened cocoa powder
½ cup chopped walnuts
2 cups miniature marshmallows
1 cup semi-sweet chocolate chips
1 cup smooth (sweetened and salted) peanut butter
1½ cups puffed rice cereal

Yield: 24 brownies

Preheat the oven to 350° F. Grease a 9-inch by 13-inch pan.

Beat together the butter or margarine and sugar until fluffy. Beat in the eggs and vanilla.

Combine the flour, baking powder, and cocoa powder. Add to the egg mixture, beating until smooth. Fold in the walnuts. Spread the batter into the prepared pan and bake for 15 minutes. Remove from the oven.

Sprinkle the marshmallows evenly on top of the brownies; bake for 3 minutes more. Place the pan on a wire rack and allow to cool.

In a small saucepan, melt the chocolate chips and peanut butter over low heat. Stir until smooth. Gently fold in the cereal. Spread the mixture on top of the cooled brownies and allow the topping to cool before cutting into squares.

Quick Turtle Brownies

Turtles—the candy kind—are pecan-studded caramels covered in rich chocolate, and they were my inspiration for these brownies. This recipe is particularly easy because it starts with a cake mix.

1 (18.25-ounce) box German chocolate
   cake mix
⅔ cup evaporated milk
¾ cup butter or margarine, melted
1 cup chopped pecans
1 cup semi-sweet chocolate chips
1 (14-ounce) bag individually wrapped
   caramels (about 50 pieces)

Preheat the oven to 350° F. Grease a 9-inch by 13-inch pan.

Mix together the cake mix, ⅓ cup of the evaporated milk, the melted butter or margarine, and pecans. Spread half the batter in the prepared pan. Bake for 6 minutes. Remove from the oven. Sprinkle the chocolate chips over the hot bottom crust.

Unwrap the caramels and melt with the remaining ⅓ cup evaporated milk over low heat, stirring constantly. Drizzle the caramel mixture over the brownies, then spoon the remaining batter over all. Return to the oven and bake for 15 to 18 minutes. Place the pan on a wire rack and allow to cool completely before cutting into squares.

Yield: 24 brownies

Mae's Triple Chocolate Quick Brownies

My Aunt Mae used to bake a pan of these brownies before almost every family camping trip. An extremely easy recipe, these brownies are still a family favorite.

1 (3½-ounce) package chocolate pudding mix (not instant)
1 (18.25-ounce) box devils food cake mix
½ cup semi-sweet chocolate chips
½ cup chopped walnuts or pecans

Preheat the oven to 350° F. Grease a 9-inch by 13-inch pan.

In medium-size saucepan, cook the pudding as the package directs.

While the pudding is still hot, combine with the cake mix, mixing well. Spread the batter in the prepared pan. Sprinkle with the chocolate chips and nuts. Bake for 30 to 35 minutes. Place on a wire rack and allow to cool completely before cutting into squares.

Yield: 24 brownies

Chocolate Brownie Torte

A thin, rich chocolate glaze tops this brownie dessert. It is easy to make, yet impressive to serve.

Torte

½ cup butter or margarine
½ cup light corn syrup
5 ounces semi-sweet baking chocolate
¾ cup sugar
1 teaspoon vanilla extract
3 eggs
1 cup all-purpose flour
1 cup chopped pecans

Glaze

3 ounces semi-sweet baking chocolate
2 teaspoons butter or margarine
2 tablespoons light corn syrup
1 teaspoon milk

Yield: 8 servings

Preheat the oven to 350° F. Grease an 8-inch round cake pan. Line the bottom of the pan with parchment or waxed paper, cut to size. Grease the paper.

In a large saucepan, bring the butter or margarine and corn syrup to a boil, stirring constantly. Add the 5 ounces chocolate and stir until melted. Add the sugar and vanilla, mixing well. Remove from the heat and set aside to cool.

When the chocolate mixture is cool, beat in the eggs, one at a time, until the mixture is smooth. Gradually add the flour, beating until smooth. Fold in the pecans. Spread the batter in the prepared pan and bake for 30 minutes. Remove from the oven and cool in the pan on a wire rack for 10 minutes. Remove

from the pan, turning onto a wire rack. Peel off the paper. Cool completely while you prepare the glaze.

Melt the remaining 3 ounces semi-sweet chocolate with the 2 teaspoons butter or margarine over low heat, stirring constantly. Add the 2 tablespoons corn syrup and milk. Stir until very smooth.

Turn the brownie right-side up on the wire rack and place a plate under the rack. Pour the glaze on the top and spread along the sides of the cooled brownie. The glaze will drip off the sides. Allow the glaze to set, then gently transfer the brownie to a serving plate.

Sweetheart Brownie Torte

This torte is my husband's favorite dessert, hence the name. The addition of sour cream results in a smooth, rich texture.

Torte

½ cup butter or margarine, softened
¾ cup sugar
1 egg
1 teaspoon vanilla extract
¾ cup sour cream
1 cup all-purpose flour
¼ cup unsweetened cocoa powder
½ teaspoon baking powder
½ teaspoon baking soda

Chocolate Glaze

½ cup semi-sweet chocolate chips
3 tablespoons butter or margarine
2 teaspoons light corn syrup

Yield: 8 servings

Preheat the oven to 350° F. Grease an 8-inch round cake pan. Line the bottom of the pan with parchment or waxed paper cut to size. Grease the paper.

In a large bowl, beat together the butter or margarine and sugar. Add the egg, vanilla, and sour cream, mixing well.

Combine the flour, cocoa powder, baking powder, and baking soda. Add to egg mixture, beating until the batter is smooth. Spread the batter in the prepared pan and bake for 30 to 35 minutes. Place the pan on a wire rack and cool for 15 minutes. Carefully remove the cake from the pan, turning it onto a wire rack. Peel off the paper and let cool completely.

To prepare the glaze, combine the chocolate chips and the remaining 3 tablespoons but-

ter or margarine and 2 teaspoons corn syrup in a saucepan over low heat. Stir constantly until the chocolate chips are melted. Remove from the heat, but continue to stir frequently, until the mixture cools and thickens slightly.

Turn the torte right-side up on the wire rack and place a plate under the rack. Spoon the cooled glaze over the top and along the sides of the cooled torte. (The glaze will drip off the sides.) Decorate, if desired, with chocolate shavings. Carefully transfer the torte to a serving plate and serve.

Coffee Brownie Torte

Coffee-flavored liqueur and almonds make a lavishly rich torte. Serve with rich, freshly brewed coffee and you will have the perfect end to a dinner party.

Torte

3 eggs
1 cup sugar
3 tablespoons coffee-flavored liqueur
2 cups finely crushed graham cracker crumbs
1 teaspoon baking powder
¾ cup chopped almonds
1 cup semi-sweet chocolate chips

Coffee Frosting

1 cup whipping cream
2 tablespoons confectioners' sugar
¼ cup coffee-flavored liqueur

Yield: 10 servings

Preheat the oven to 350° F. Grease a 9-inch springform pan.

In a large bowl, beat together the eggs and sugar until frothy. Add the 3 tablespoons coffee liqueur and continue beating until smooth.

Combine the graham cracker crumbs and baking powder. Add to the egg mixture, mixing well. Fold in the almonds and chocolate chips. Spread the batter in the prepared pan and bake for 30 minutes. Place the pan on a wire rack and allow to cool completely.

To make the frosting, beat together all ingredients with an electric mixer until stiff peaks form. Carefully remove the sides of the springform pan and transfer the torte to a serving plate. Spread the frosting on the torte and serve.

2
Fruit and Nut Bars

Fruit and nut bars can be prepared in minutes, they bake quickly and can be served on any occasion. Some of the recipes here even start with the convenience of a packaged cake mix but the results taste completely homemade.

Mouth-watering Apple-Cheese Pleasers and Lemon Bars are excellent fruit bar choices, while Pecan Cookie Bars and Almond Bars round out the nut bar collection. Some of the recipes consist of both fruit and nuts, enabling one to sample the best of both worlds.

I included in this collection bars made with good-for-you oats, wheat germ, and granola, thereby ensuring a guilt-free take-along breakfast to eat on your way out the door in the morning. These wholesome bars are handy to have around when mid-morning hunger pangs hit at school or the office, and the only snack available is an overly sweet danish off the coffee cart.

Experiment! Use walnuts when pecans are called for, leave out or add raisins. With a little imagination, the recipes in this section can become an even larger collection.

Unless otherwise specified, fruit and nut bars can be stored, covered, in the pan in which they were baked for several days. Refrigerate for storage up to a week. Some bars can also be frozen, individually wrapped, for up to 3 months. Whether a specific bar freezes well is indicated in the recipe.

Almond Shortbread

Perfect with after-dinner coffee or espresso, these buttery triangles melt in your mouth. Please use only butter—not margarine—in these. The simplicity of the ingredients demand the real taste of butter.

1¼ cups butter, softened
⅔ cup sugar
1 cup finely chopped almonds
½ teaspoon almond extract
3 cups all-purpose flour

Preheat the oven to 325° F.

Beat together the butter and sugar until light and fluffy. Add ½ cup of the almonds and the almond extract, mixing until creamy. Add the flour, mixing well. Press the mixture evenly into an ungreased 10-inch by 15-inch baking pan. Sprinkle with the remaining ½ cup almonds and gently press them into the dough. Bake for about 25 minutes, or until the shortbread turns a light golden color and is firm in the center when lightly pressed.

Immediately cut the shortbread into 3-inch squares, then cut each square diagonally in half. Allow the shortbread triangles to cool in the pan on a wire rack. Remove gently from the pan with a wide spatula. Store in an airtight container.

Yield: 30 shortbread

Pecan Bars

Crunchy pecan pieces are embedded in the top and bottom crusts and butterscotch chips add a creamy, chewy texture between the layers.

½ cup butter or margarine, softened
½ cup white sugar
1½ cups firmly packed brown sugar
2 eggs, separated and at room
   temperature
1 teaspoon vanilla extract
2 cups all-purpose flour
1 teaspoon baking soda
¼ teaspoon salt
1 cup chopped pecans
1 cup butterscotch chips

Preheat the oven to 325° F. Grease a 9-inch by 13-inch pan.

Cream together the butter or margarine, white sugar, and ½ cup of the brown sugar until fluffy. Add the egg yolks and vanilla.

Mix together the flour, baking soda, and salt. Add to the egg mixture, mixing well. The dough will be stiff. Press the dough into the bottom of the prepared pan. Sprinkle ½ cup of the pecans and all of the butterscotch chips over the dough and pat in gently.

In separate bowl, beat the egg whites until soft peaks form. Gradually add the remaining 1 cup brown sugar and beat until stiff peaks form. Spread over the dough and sprinkle with the remaining ½ cup pecans. Bake for 40 to 45 minutes. Cut into bars while warm.

Yield: 24 bars

Coffee Bars

A perfect accompaniment to a mid-morning cup of coffee, Coffee Bars have a subtle coffee flavor all their own.

½ cup butter or margarine, softened
1 cup firmly packed brown sugar
1 egg
1 teaspoon vanilla extract
½ cup very strong cold brewed coffee
1½ cups all-purpose flour
½ teaspoon baking powder
½ teaspoon baking soda
1 teaspoon cinnamon
1 cup raisins
¼ cup chopped walnuts
Confectioners' sugar

Preheat the oven to 350° F. Grease a 9-inch by 13-inch pan.

Beat together the butter or margarine and brown sugar until fluffy. Add the egg, vanilla, and coffee, mixing well.

In separate bowl, combine the flour, baking powder, baking soda, and cinnamon. Add to the egg mixture, mixing well. Fold in the raisins and walnuts. Spread in the prepared pan and bake for 25 to 30 minutes. Place the pan on a wire rack and allow to cool completely. Sprinkle with confectioners' sugar. Cut into bars.

Yield: 24 bars

Blondies

These squares taste like everyone's favorite chocolate chip cookie.

¾ cup butter or margarine
1 cup sugar
2 eggs
½ teaspoon vanilla extract
2 cups all-purpose flour
1 teaspoon baking soda
¼ teaspoon salt
¼ teaspoon cinnamon
1 cup semi-sweet chocolate chips
½ cup chopped walnuts

Preheat the oven to 350° F. Grease a 9-inch by 13-inch pan.

Beat together the butter or margarine and sugar until fluffy. Add the eggs and the vanilla, mixing well.

In a separate bowl, combine the flour, baking soda, salt, and cinnamon. Add to the egg mixture, mixing well. Fold in the chocolate chips and nuts. Spread the batter in the prepared pan and bake for 30 to 40 minutes. Place the pan on a wire rack and allow to cool completely before cutting into squares. These bars freeze well.

Yield: 24 squares

Butterscotch Bars

Sweetened with dark brown sugar and crunchy with nuts, these bars are absolutely delicious!

½ cup butter or margarine
1 cup firmly packed dark brown sugar
1 egg
1 teaspoon vanilla extract
½ cup all-purpose flour
1 teaspoon baking powder
¼ teaspoon salt
¾ cup chopped walnuts or pecans

Preheat the oven to 350° F. Grease an 8-inch square pan.

Beat together the butter or margarine and sugar until fluffy. Add the egg and vanilla, mixing well.

In a separate bowl, combine the flour, baking powder, and salt. Add to egg mixture, mixing well. Fold in the nuts. Spread in the prepared pan and bake for 25 minutes. Place the pan on a wire rack and allow to cool completely before cutting into bars. These bars freeze well.

Yield: 16 bars

Blarney Stones

Blarney Stones

4 eggs, separated and at room
    temperature
1½ cups sugar
⅛ teaspoon salt
2 cups all-purpose flour
½ teaspoon baking soda
1 teaspoon cream of tartar
½ cup cold water

Icing

1 cup butter or margarine
1 (16-ounce) package confectioners'
    sugar
1 teaspoon vanilla extract
2 tablespoons milk
1½ cups finely chopped roasted, salted
    peanuts

Yield: 32 cookies

Preheat the oven to 350° F. Grease two 8-inch square pans.

Beat the egg yolks. Add the sugar and salt and continue beating until well mixed. Set aside.

In a medium-size bowl, combine the flour, baking soda, and cream of tartar. Add the dry ingredients to the egg yolk mixture alternately with the cold water, beating until the batter is smooth. Set aside.

In a separate bowl, beat the egg whites until stiff. Gently fold into the batter. Spread the batter in the prepared pans. Bake for 25 to 30 minutes. Place the pans on wire racks and allow to cool completely before cutting into squares.

To prepare the icing, beat together the but-

ter or margarine, confectioners' sugar, vanilla, and milk. The icing should be very thin. One at a time, dip each Blarney Stone in the icing, then immediately roll in the peanuts. Store in an airtight container.

Peanut Butter Squares

A batch of peanut butter cookies made easy—and fast!

5 tablespoons butter or margarine
¾ cup crunchy or smooth (sweetened and salted) peanut butter
2 eggs
1 cup sugar
1 teaspoon vanilla extract
½ cup all-purpose flour
¼ teaspoon baking powder

Preheat the oven to 350° F. Grease an 8-inch square pan.

Melt the butter or margarine over low heat. Stir in the peanut butter. Remove from the heat and allow to cool slightly.

Beat together the eggs and sugar until frothy. Add the vanilla. Add the peanut butter mixture, mixing until smooth.

Combine the flour and baking powder. Add to the peanut butter mixture, beating until smooth. Spread the batter in the prepared pan and bake for 25 minutes. Place on a wire rack and allow to cool completely before cutting into squares. These squares freeze well.

Yield: 16 squares

Peanut Butter Marble Bars

Peanut butter and chocolate—two favorite flavors combined in one moist cookie bar.

½ cup smooth (sweetened and salted) peanut butter
⅓ cup butter or margarine, softened
¾ cup firmly packed brown sugar
¾ cup white sugar
2 eggs
2 teaspoons vanilla extract
1 cup all-purpose flour
1 teaspoon baking powder
2 cups semi-sweet chocolate chips

Preheat the oven to 350° F. Grease a 9-inch by 13-inch pan.

Beat together the peanut butter, butter or margarine, and sugars until fluffy. Add the eggs and vanilla, mixing well.

Combine the flour and baking powder and add to the peanut butter mixture, beating until smooth. Spread the batter in the prepared pan.

Melt the chocolate chips over very low heat. Drop spoonfuls of the melted chocolate on top of the batter in the pan. Zigzag a knife or spatula through the batter to marble in the chocolate. Bake for 25 to 30 minutes. Place the pan on a wire rack and allow to cool completely before cutting into bars. These bars freeze well.

Yield: 24 bars

Peanut Butter Oat Squares

Chewy with oats and coconut, these peanutty bars have the peanut butter spread on top, rather than inside the bar.

2 cups all-purpose flour
2 cups rolled oats (regular or quick)
1½ cups firmly packed brown sugar
⅔ cup sweetened shredded coconut
½ cup chopped roasted, salted peanuts
1 cup butter or margarine, melted
1 cup smooth (sweetened and salted)
  peanut butter

Preheat the oven to 350° F. Grease a 9-inch by 13-inch pan.

In a large bowl, combine the flour, oats, brown sugar, coconut, and peanuts. Pour in the melted butter or margarine and mix well. The mixture will be crumbly. Gently press the mixture into the prepared pan. Bake for 20 minutes, or 25 minutes if a crispier bar is desired.

Remove from the oven and let cool slightly. While still warm, spread the peanut butter evenly over the crust. Place the pan on a wire rack and allow to cool completely before cutting into bars.

Yield: 24 bars

Oatmeal Carrot Bars

Made with healthy ingredients, these bars are best served still warm from the oven, topped with a scoop of frozen raspberry or vanilla yogurt.

⅓ cup butter or margarine, softened
1 cup firmly packed brown sugar
1 egg
1 teaspoon vanilla extract
¾ cup finely shredded carrot
½ cup all-purpose flour
½ cup whole wheat flour
½ cup rolled oats (regular or quick)
¼ cup toasted wheat germ
1 teaspoon baking powder
⅛ teaspoon salt
½ cup raisins

Yield: 24 bars

Preheat the oven to 350° F. Grease an 8-inch square pan.

Cream together the butter or margarine and brown sugar. Add the egg and vanilla, mixing well. Fold in the shredded carrot.

Combine the flours, oats, wheat germ, baking powder, and salt. Add to the carrot mixture, mixing well. Fold in the raisins. Spread the batter in the prepared pan and bake for 30 to 35 minutes. Place the pan on a wire rack and cool for at least 10 minutes before cutting into bars.

Granola Bars

Granola Bars make a chewy, wholesome snack, full of the goodness of oats, raisins, nuts, and honey.

3½ cups rolled oats (regular or quick)
⅔ cup butter or margarine, softened
½ cup firmly packed brown sugar
⅓ cup honey
1 egg
½ teaspoon vanilla extract
¼ teaspoon salt
1 cup raisins
½ cup sweetened shredded coconut
¾ cup coarsely chopped walnuts or
    pecans

Preheat the oven to 350° F. Grease a 15-inch by 10-inch pan.

Spread the oats evenly on an ungreased cookie sheet or jelly roll pan. Toast in the oven for approximately 15 minutes. Remove from the oven and set aside to cool.

Beat the butter or margarine with the brown sugar and honey until fluffy. Add the egg and vanilla, mixing well. Add the toasted oats, salt, raisins, coconut, and nuts, mixing well. Press the mixture into the prepared pan. Bake for 15 to 20 minutes. Place the pan on a wire rack and allow to cool completely before cutting into bars. These bars freeze well.

Yield: 30 bars

Apricot-Granola Treats

These granola bars taste almost too good to be good for you. But with the protein from the eggs, grains, and nonfat milk, and the iron and potassium from the apricots, these treats are worth eating.

1 cup butter or margarine, softened
1½ cups firmly packed brown sugar
2 eggs
1 teaspoon vanilla extract
1¾ cups all-purpose flour
½ cup toasted wheat germ
½ cup nonfat dry milk powder
1 teaspoon baking soda
½ teaspoon salt
1¾ cups granola (store-bought or homemade)
¼ cup sesame seeds
1 cup chopped dried apricots

Yield: 24 bars

Preheat the oven to 350° F. Generously grease a 9-inch by 13-inch pan.

Beat together the butter or margarine and brown sugar until fluffy. Add the eggs and vanilla, mixing well.

In a separate bowl, combine the flour, wheat germ, dry milk, baking soda, salt, granola, and sesame seeds. Gradually add to the egg mixture, mixing well. Fold in the apricots. Spread the batter in the prepared pan and bake for 25 to 30 minutes. Place the pan on a wire rack and allow to cool completely before cutting into bars. These bars freeze well.

Banana Granola Bars

These granola bars are soft, cake-like, and not too sweet.

⅓ cup butter or margarine, softened
½ cup sugar
¼ cup unsulphured molasses
1 egg
1⅓ cups mashed ripe bananas
¼ cup nonfat dry milk powder
1¼ cups all-purpose flour
1 cup rolled oats (regular or quick)
1 teaspoon baking powder
¼ teaspoon baking soda
¼ teaspoon ground ginger
½ teaspoon grated lemon rind
½ cup sweetened shredded coconut
2 tablespoons sesame seeds
½ cup raisins

Yield: 24 bars

Preheat the oven to 375° F. Grease a 9-inch by 13-inch pan.

Beat together the butter or margarine, sugar, and molasses until fluffy. Beat in the egg, bananas, and dry milk.

Combine the flour, oats, baking powder, baking soda, and ginger. Add to the egg mixture, mixing well. Fold in the lemon rind, coconut, sesame seeds, and raisins. Spread in the prepared pan and bake for 20 to 25 minutes, or until the center springs back when lightly touched. Place the pan on a wire rack and allow to cool completely before cutting into bars. These bars freeze well.

Caramel Granola Bars

Because these bars are especially rich, I suggest you cut them into small bars.

¾ cup butter or margarine, softened
¾ cup confectioners' sugar
1½ cups all-purpose flour
2 eggs
1½ cups firmly packed brown sugar
1 teaspoon vanilla extract
2 cups granola (store-bought or homemade)
2 tablespoons all-purpose flour
½ teaspoon baking powder
¼ teaspoon salt

Preheat the oven to 350° F.

In a large bowl, beat together the butter or margarine and confectioners' sugar until fluffy. Gradually mix in 1½ cups flour. Press the mixture into the bottom of an ungreased 9-inch by 13-inch pan. Bake for 12 minutes, or until lightly browned. Remove from oven and allow to cool slightly on a wire rack.

Beat together the eggs and brown sugar until frothy. Add the vanilla.

Combine the granola, the remaining 2 tablespoons flour, baking powder, and salt. Add to the egg mixture, mixing well. Spread the granola mixture over the baked crust, return to the oven, and bake for an additional 20 minutes, or until the edges are lightly browned. Place on a wire rack and allow to cool completely before cutting into bars.

Yield: 36 bars

Raisin Oat Squares

A cake-like, wholesome bar, chewy with raisins and crunchy with nuts.

1 cup rolled oats (regular or quick)
¾ cup all-purpose flour
½ teaspoon baking powder
½ cup raisins
½ cup chopped walnuts or pecans
½ teaspoon cinnamon
¼ teaspoon ground nutmeg
¾ cup firmly packed brown sugar
¼ cup vegetable oil
¼ cup milk
1 egg
1 teaspoon vanilla extract

Preheat the oven to 350° F. Grease an 8-inch square pan.

In a medium-size bowl, combine the oats, flour, baking powder, raisins, nuts, cinnamon, and nutmeg. Set aside.

In a small bowl, mix the brown sugar, oil, milk, egg, and vanilla. Add to the oat mixture, mixing well. Spread the batter in the prepared pan and bake for 25 to 30 minutes. Place on a wire rack and allow to cool completely before cutting into squares.

Yield: 16 squares

Raisin Bran Spice Bars

Chewy with the goodness of raisins and bran, these bars are a healthy alternative to a candy bar. Perfect for lunch boxes and after-school snacks.

1 cup water
1 cup raisins
¾ cup bran cereal (not flakes)
½ cup vegetable oil
1 egg
1 cup all-purpose flour
⅔ cup sugar
1 teaspoon cinnamon
¼ teaspoon ground nutmeg
¼ teaspoon ground cloves
¼ teaspoon salt
½ cup chopped pecans
Confectioners' sugar

Yield: 30 bars

Preheat the oven to 375° F. Grease a 9-inch by 13-inch pan.

In a medium-size saucepan, combine the water and raisins. Bring to a boil over medium heat. Remove from the heat and spoon the raisins into a large bowl. Stir in the bran cereal and vegetable oil. Set aside to cool. When the mixture is cool, beat in the egg.

In medium-size bowl, combine the flour, sugar, cinnamon, nutmeg, cloves, and salt. Add to the raisin mixture, mixing well. Fold in the pecans. Spread the batter evenly in the prepared pan. Bake for 25 minutes, or until a tester inserted in the center comes out clean. Place on a wire rack and allow to cool completely.

Sprinkle the top with sifted confectioners' sugar. Cut into bars. These bars freeze well.

Apple Pecan Squares

⅔ cup butter or margarine, softened
2 cups firmly packed brown sugar
2 eggs
1 teaspoon vanilla extract
2 cups all-purpose flour
2 teaspoons baking powder
1 cup peeled and diced apple
½ cup chopped pecans
Confectioners' sugar

Preheat the oven to 350° F. Grease a 9-inch by 13-inch pan.

Beat together the butter or margarine and sugar until fluffy. Add the eggs and vanilla, mixing well.

Combine the flour and baking powder. Add to the egg mixture and beat until the batter is smooth. Fold in the apples and pecans. Spread the batter in the prepared pan and bake for 25 to 30 minutes. Place on a wire rack and allow to cool completely.

Dust the top with sifted confectioners' sugar. Cut into squares.

Yield: 24 squares

Apple-Cheese Pleasers

The cheese taste is subtle; it adds a rich tang to the cookie. Try these bars for a quick, on-the-go breakfast with a glass of milk. They are high in protein and kids love them.

⅔ cup butter or margarine, softened
⅓ cup firmly packed brown sugar
1 egg
1 teaspoon vanilla extract
¾ cup all-purpose flour
1½ cups rolled oats (regular or quick)
½ teaspoon baking powder
½ teaspoon cinnamon
½ teaspoon salt
1½ cups shredded cheddar cheese
1 cup peeled and diced apple

Preheat the oven to 350° F. Grease an 8-inch square pan.

In a large bowl, beat together the butter or margarine and brown sugar until fluffy. Add the egg and vanilla, mixing well.

Combine the flour, oats, baking powder, cinnamon, and salt. Add to the egg mixture, mixing well. Gradually add the shredded cheese and mix well. Fold in the diced apple. Spread the batter in the prepared pan. Bake for 25 minutes or until the top is golden brown. Place the pan on a wire rack and allow to cool completely before cutting into squares.

Yield: 16 squares

Yogurt Apple Bars

These bars are sweet-tart in flavor, thanks to the yogurt and lemon.

¼ cup butter or margarine, melted
1½ cups finely crushed graham cracker crumbs
1 (14-ounce) can sweetened condensed milk
1 cup plain yogurt
½ teaspoon grated lemon rind
2 tablespoons fresh lemon juice
3 cups peeled and diced apple
Cinnamon

Preheat the oven to 350° F. Grease a 9-inch by 13-inch pan.

Combine the melted butter or margarine and graham cracker crumbs. Pat the mixture into the bottom of the prepared pan. Set aside.

Mix together the condensed milk, yogurt, lemon rind, and lemon juice. Set aside and allow the mixture to thicken slightly.

Evenly distribute the diced apple over the crust in the pan. Pour the yogurt mixture over the apples. Bake for 25 minutes.

Remove from oven and dust lightly with cinnamon. Cool completely on a wire rack before cutting into bars.

Yield: 24 bars

Apricot Bars

¾ cup chopped dried apricots
1 cup water
1 cup butter or margarine, softened
1½ cups sugar
2 eggs
3 cups all-purpose flour
1¼ teaspoons baking soda
½ teaspoon salt
½ teaspoon cinnamon

Preheat the oven to 350° F. Grease an 18-inch by 12-inch jelly roll pan.

Boil the apricots in the water until the liquid is almost completely absorbed and the mixture is thickened. Set aside to cool.

Beat together the butter or margarine and sugar until creamy. Add the eggs, mixing well. Stir in the cooled apricots.

Combine the flour, baking soda, salt, and cinnamon. Add to the egg mixture, mixing well. Spread the batter in the prepared pan and bake for 15 to 20 minutes.

Remove from the oven and sprinkle the bars with additional cinnamon while warm, if desired. Allow to cool completely before cutting into bars. These freeze well.

Yield: 30 bars

Cherry Squares

Cherry and chocolate make a delicious combination.

½ cup butter or margarine, softened
½ cup firmly packed brown sugar
½ cup white sugar
2 eggs
1 tablespoon vanilla extract
2 cups all-purpose flour
1½ teaspoons baking powder
½ teaspoon salt
¾ cup milk
1 cup chopped walnuts
1 cup drained chopped maraschino
  cherries
1 cup mini semi-sweet chocolate chips

Preheat the oven to 325° F. Grease a 9-inch by 13-inch pan.

Beat together the butter or margarine and sugars until fluffy. Add the eggs and vanilla, mixing well.

Combine the flour, baking powder, and salt. Add to the egg mixture alternately with the milk. Fold in the walnuts, cherries, and chocolate chips. Spread the mixture in the prepared pan and bake for 25 minutes. Place on a wire rack and allow to cool completely before cutting into squares. These squares freeze well.

Yield: 24 squares

Cranberry-Prune Squares

¼ cup butter or margarine, softened
1 cup sugar
2 eggs
1 cup all-purpose flour
½ teaspoon baking powder
½ teaspoon cinnamon
½ teaspoon ground cloves
½ teaspoon allspice
1 cup chopped pecans
1 cup chopped prunes
1 cup fresh or frozen whole cranberries

Preheat the oven to 350° F. Grease an 8-inch square pan.

Beat together the butter or margarine and sugar until fluffy. Add the eggs, mixing well.

Combine the flour, baking powder, and spices. Add to the egg mixture, mixing well. Gently fold in the pecans, prunes, and cranberries. Spread the batter in the prepared pan and bake for about 45 minutes, or until the center feels firm when lightly touched and the edges begin to pull away from the pan. Place on a wire rack and allow to cool completely before cutting into squares.

Yield: 16 squares

Date Bars

Here's a classic—an intensely sweet, chewy bar.

3 eggs
1 cup sugar
1 teaspoon vanilla extract
1 cup all-purpose flour
1 teaspoon baking powder
¼ teaspoon salt
1½ cups sliced pitted dates
1 cup chopped walnuts or pecans
Confectioners' sugar

Preheat the oven to 350° F. Grease a 9-inch by 13-inch pan.

Beat the eggs until light and fluffy. Add the sugar and continue beating. Add the vanilla.

Combine the flour, baking powder, and salt. Add to the egg mixture, beating until the batter is smooth. Fold in the dates and nuts. Spread the batter in the prepared pan and bake for 30 minutes.

Remove from oven and allow to cool slightly on a wire rack. Cut into bars while warm and roll in confectioners' sugar. Store in an airtight container.

Yield: 24 bars

Persimmon Spice Squares

A fully ripe persimmon can be sweet and rich-tasting, but an underripe one will make your mouth pucker with its tartness. Look for soft fruit, with cap and stem intact; it is okay if the skin is wrinkled. Cut through the tough skin, peel the skin back, and then use the pulp.

½ cup butter or margarine, softened
1 cup sugar
1 egg
1 cup persimmon pulp, sieved
2 cups all-purpose flour
1 teaspoon baking powder
1 teaspoon baking soda
½ teaspoon cinnamon
½ teaspoon ground nutmeg
1 cup raisins or dried currants
1 cup coarsely chopped walnuts

Yield: 24 squares

Preheat the oven to 350° F. Grease a 9-inch by 13-inch pan.

Beat together the butter or margarine and sugar until fluffy. Add the egg and persimmon pulp, mixing well.

Combine the flour, baking powder, baking soda, cinnamon, and nutmeg. Add to the egg mixture, mixing well. Fold in the raisins or currants and walnuts. Spread the mixture in the prepared pan. Bake for 20 to 25 minutes. Place the pan on a wire rack and allow to cool completely before cutting into squares.

Coconut Cookie Bars

A cookie-like crust is covered with a sweet, creamy coconut topping, then baked to a golden brown crunchy bar.

½ cup butter or margarine, melted
1 (18.25-ounce) box yellow cake mix
3 eggs
1 (8-ounce) package cream cheese, softened
1 (16-ounce) package confectioners' sugar
¾ cup sweetened shredded coconut
½ cup chopped pecans

Preheat the oven to 325° F. Grease a 10-inch by 15-inch jelly roll pan.

Combine the butter or margarine, cake mix, and 1 of the eggs. Mix together until crumbly. Press the mixture into the bottom of the prepared pan. Set aside.

Beat together the cream cheese and sugar until smooth. Add the remaining 2 eggs, mixing well. Fold in the coconut and pecans. Pour the cream cheese mixture over the crumb mixture, spreading evenly. Bake for 45 to 50 minutes, or until golden brown. Place the pan on a wire rack and allow to cool completely before cutting into bars.

Yield: 40 bars

Cheesecake Squares

Here is real, creamy cheesecake in bar form—a nutty brown sugar crust with a sweet, smooth filling.

⅔ cup firmly packed brown sugar
1 cup chopped pecans
2 cups all-purpose flour
⅔ cup butter or margarine, melted
2 (8-ounce) packages cream cheese, softened
½ cup white sugar
2 eggs
2 tablespoons lemon juice
¼ cup milk
2 teaspoons vanilla extract

Preheat the oven to 325° F. Grease a 9-inch by 13-inch pan.

Combine the brown sugar, pecans, and flour in a medium-size bowl. Add the melted butter or margarine, mixing until crumbly. Set aside 1 cup of this crumb mixture. Press the remaining crumbs into the bottom of the prepared pan. Bake for 12 minutes. Remove from the oven and set aside to cool slightly.

Beat together the cream cheese, white sugar, eggs, lemon juice, milk, and vanilla until creamy. Spread over the crust. Sprinkle the reserved crumbs over the top. Bake for an additional 25 minutes. Place the pan on a wire rack and allow to cool completely before cutting into squares. Store in the refrigerator.

Yield: 24 squares

Almond Bars

Almond Bars are perfect for holiday giving. Fill a decorative tin with these rich dessert bars and present them to the special ones on your Christmas list.

Crust

¾ cup white sugar
2 cups all-purpose flour
⅔ cup butter or margarine, chilled
1 egg
½ teaspoon almond extract

Filling

¼ cup butter or margarine, softened
½ cup white sugar
2 eggs
½ teaspoon almond extract
½ cup finely ground almonds
Confectioners' sugar

Yield: 30 bars

Preheat the oven to 350° F.

To make the crust, mix together the sugar and flour. With 2 knives or a pastry blender, work in the butter or margarine until the mixture resembles coarse crumbs. Add the egg and almond extract and mix until a soft dough forms. Press the dough into the bottom of a 9-inch by 13-inch pan.

To make the filling, beat together the butter or margarine and sugar until fluffy. Add the eggs and almond extract, mixing well. Fold in the ground almonds. Pour the egg mixture over dough, spreading evenly. Bake for 25 to 30 minutes, or until the filling is golden brown and set. Place the pan on a wire rack and allow to cool completely.

Dust with confectioners' sugar. Cut into bars. These freeze well.

Layered Apple Butter Bars

To make apple butter, cook some quartered apples in a little water to soften, then press through a food mill to puree and remove the peels and cores. Pour the apple puree into a shallow baking dish or roasting pan and bake for 4 to 6 hours at 300° F., stirring from time to time, until so thick you can run a spoon through it, leaving a visible trail. Sweeten to taste with sugar, honey, or maple syrup.

¼ cup butter or margarine
⅔ cup firmly packed dark brown sugar
1 cup all-purpose flour
1 cup rolled oats (regular or quick)
¼ teaspoon baking soda
¼ teaspoon salt
1 cup sweetened or unsweetened apple
   butter
⅔ cup coarsely chopped walnuts

Yield: 16 bars

Preheat the oven to 350° F. Grease an 8-inch square pan.

Beat together the butter and sugar until fluffy. Set aside.

Combine the flour, oats, baking soda, and salt. Add to the butter mixture, mixing well. The mixture will be crumbly. Lightly press 2 cups of the oat mixture into the bottom of the prepared pan. Spread the apple butter evenly over the crust. Mix the walnuts with the remaining oat mixture and sprinkle over the apple butter layer. Bake for 25 to 30 minutes, or until the top is lightly browned. Place the pan on a wire rack and allow to cool completely before cutting into bars. These bars freeze well.

Crunchy Apple Coconut Bars

In this cookie, apples are sandwiched between a buttery shortbread crust and a sweet coconut topping.

Crust

⅓ cup butter or margarine, softened
3 tablespoons brown sugar
1 cup all-purpose flour

Filling

2 teaspoons butter or margarine
¼ cup white sugar
3 cups sliced peeled apples
2 tablespoons fresh lemon juice
½ teaspoon grated lemon rind

Topping

3 tablespoons butter or margarine, melted
¾ cup white sugar
1 egg
1 cup sweetened shredded coconut
½ cup chopped pecans

Preheat the oven to 350° F.

To make the crust, cream together the butter or margarine and brown sugar until fluffy. Gradually mix in the flour. Pat the dough into the bottom of an ungreased 8-inch square pan.

To make the filling, combine all the filling ingredients in a medium-size saucepan. Cook over medium-high heat, stirring frequently, until thick, about 5 minutes. Remove from the heat and cool slightly.

Yield: 16 bars

To make topping, beat together the butter or margarine, sugar, and egg. Fold in the coconut and pecans.

Spread the slightly cooled filling evenly over the dough in the pan. Spread the topping over the filling. Bake for 20 to 25 minutes or until the coconut topping is golden brown. Place the pan on a wire rack and cool completely before cutting into bars.

Old-Fashioned Cherry Bars

When you sandwich tart cherries between two layers of oatmeal cookie crust, you get something better than cherry pie!

1 (16-ounce) can pitted sour cherries
  with juice
¾ cup white sugar
3 tablespoons all-purpose flour
⅔ cup butter or margarine, softened
1½ cups firmly packed brown sugar
1½ cups rolled oats (regular or quick)
1½ cups all-purpose flour
⅛ teaspoon salt

Preheat the oven to 350° F. Grease a 9-inch by 13-inch pan.

In a medium-size saucepan, combine the cherries with the white sugar and 3 tablespoons flour. Simmer over medium heat until the cherries are thickened, 3 to 5 minutes. Set aside to cool.

Combine the butter or margarine, brown sugar, oats, 1½ cups flour, and salt. The mixture will be crumbly. Press half of the oat mixture into the bottom of the prepared pan. Evenly spread the cooled cherry mixture over the oat layer, then sprinkle the top with the remaining oat mixture. Bake for 40 minutes or until the top is lightly browned. Place the pan on a wire rack and allow to cool completely before cutting into bars. These bars freeze well.

Yield: 24 bars

Lemon Bars

No collection of bar cookie recipes would be complete without Lemon Bars. These cookies achieve a perfect balance between tart and sweet.

Crust

1 cup butter or margarine, softened
½ cup confectioners' sugar
2 cups all-purpose flour
⅛ teaspoon salt

Filling

4 eggs, beaten
2 cups sugar
¼ cup all-purpose flour
6 tablespoons fresh lemon juice
Confectioners' sugar (optional)

Yield: 24 bars

Preheat the oven to 350° F. Grease a 9-inch by 13-inch pan.

Combine all the crust ingredients and press into the prepared pan. Bake for 15 minutes, remove from the oven, and let cool slightly.

To make the filling, beat together the eggs and sugar until fluffy. Gradually beat in the flour and lemon juice. Pour the lemon mixture over the slightly cooled crust. Bake for 20 to 25 minutes. Place the pan on a wire rack and allow to cool completely.

Sprinkle with additional confectioners' sugar, if desired. Cut into bars.

Macadamia Nut Bars

After visiting Hawaii, I developed these bars to keep my vacation memories alive.

Crust

½ cup butter or margarine, softened
¼ cup white sugar
1 cup all-purpose flour

Filling

2 eggs
½ cup sweetened shredded coconut
1½ cups firmly packed brown sugar
1 teaspoon vanilla extract
1 cup chopped roasted, salted macadamia nuts
2 tablespoons all-purpose flour
½ teaspoon baking powder

Yield: 24 bars

Preheat the oven to 350° F. Grease an 8-inch square pan.

To make the crust, beat together the butter or margarine and white sugar until fluffy. Gradually add the flour and mix well. Lightly press the mixture into bottom of the prepared pan and bake for 20 minutes. Remove from the oven and let cool slightly.

While the crust cools, make the filling. Beat the eggs slightly. Continue beating while adding the remaining filling ingredients, mixing well. Spread the filling mixture over the warm baked crust. Return to the oven and bake for an additional 20 minutes. Place the pan on a wire rack and allow to cool completely before cutting into bars.

Pecan Cookie Bars

This simple recipe starts with a packaged yellow cake mix, so it goes together quickly and easily. The crust is cookie-like in texture, and the crunchy filling resembles pecan pie.

Crust

1 (18.25-ounce) box yellow cake mix
½ cup butter or margarine, melted
1 egg

Filling

½ cup firmly packed brown sugar
1½ cups dark corn syrup
3 eggs
1 teaspoon vanilla extract
1 cup chopped pecans

Preheat the oven to 350° F. Grease a 9-inch by 13-inch pan.

To make the crust, pour the cake mix into a medium-size bowl. Measure out ⅔ cup of the cake mix and set aside. To the remaining mix, add the melted butter or margarine and egg, mixing well. The mixture will be crumbly. Gently press the mixture into the bottom of the prepared pan. Bake for 20 minutes.

Meanwhile, prepare the filling by combining the reserved cake mix, brown sugar, corn syrup, eggs, vanilla, and pecans. Beat together until the batter is smooth. Spread over the baked crust and return to the oven to bake for an additional 40 minutes, or until the filling is set. Place the pan on a wire rack and allow to cool completely before cutting into bars.

Yield: 24 bars

Pumpkin Pie Squares

Crust

½ cup butter or margarine, melted
½ cup firmly packed brown sugar
1 cup all-purpose flour
¾ cup rolled oats (regular or quick)

Filling

1 (16-ounce) can cooked pumpkin puree
2 eggs
1⅓ cups milk
⅔ cup white sugar
1 teaspoon cinnamon
½ teaspoon ground cloves

Topping

2 tablespoons butter or margarine, melted
½ cup firmly packed brown sugar
½ cup chopped walnuts or pecans

Preheat the oven to 350° F.

To make the crust, combine the melted butter or margarine, brown sugar, flour, and oats. Mix until crumbly. Press the mixture into the bottom of an ungreased 9-inch by 13-inch pan. Bake for 12 minutes. Remove from the oven and allow to cool slightly on a wire rack.

To make the filling, beat together the pumpkin, eggs, milk, white sugar, and spices, mixing well. Spread over the warm crust and bake for 20 minutes while you prepare the topping.

To make the topping, mix together all the

Yield: 12 squares

topping ingredients until crumbly.

After baking for 20 minutes, remove the baking pan from the oven and sprinkle the topping mixture over the pumpkin filling. Return to the oven and bake for an additional 15 to 20 minutes. Place on a wire rack and allow to cool completely before cutting into 3-inch squares. Serve with whipped cream, if desired. Store in the refrigerator.

Whole Grain Jam Squares

A layered cookie treat, wholesome with the crunch of oats, nuts, and whole wheat flour.

1 cup butter or margarine, softened
1 cup firmly packed brown sugar
1 cup all-purpose flour
¾ cup whole wheat flour
2 cups rolled oats (regular or quick)
½ teaspoon baking soda
1 teaspoon cinnamon
½ teaspoon salt
½ cup chopped almonds
¾ cup jam or preserves

Preheat the oven to 400° F. Grease a 9-inch by 13-inch pan.

Combine all the ingredients, except the jam or preserves, in a large bowl, mixing well. The mixture will be crumbly.

Press half of the mixture into the bottom of the prepared pan. Spread the jam or preserves over, then sprinkle the reserved oat mixture over the jam. Bake for 25 to 30 minutes or until the top is golden brown. Place the pan on a wire rack and allow to cool completely before cutting into squares. These squares freeze well.

Yield: 24 squares

3
Biscotti

Biscotti are dry-crisp Italian cookies that look a bit like small slices of toasted bread. The "bis" means twice and the "cotti" means cooked—and the crunchy cookies contained in this section call for just that.

The biscotti dough is first shaped into a log, then baked until lightly browned. The logs are allowed to cool for a few minutes, then sliced on the diagonal. The slices are then returned to the oven for a second baking, which results in an extremely crisp, rather hard cookie. After cooling, biscotti can be stored in airtight containers for up to 2 months. They will keep for a few months in the freezer as well.

Biscotti are cookies that are perfect for dipping. If milk and coffee are all that come to mind, imagine these slightly sweet, crunchy biscuits as an irresistible accompaniment to an after-dinner cup of espresso or cappucino. Almost any hot beverage is delicious with biscotti, and the Italians occasionally enjoy biscotti dunked in a sweet dessert wine.

Biscotti have long been offered in Italian bakeries across the country. They are now available in espresso bars and restaurants throughout larger metropolitan cities, such as New York, Los Angeles, and San Francisco. On the West Coast, supermarkets and delis are offering them.

From this section you'll learn to bake biscotti just as delectable as those sold in family-owned bakeries. From Basic Biscotti to biscotti spiced with ginger or spiked with citrus, the recipes are easy, and the results—crisp and delicious!

Basic Biscotti

These are the plainest of biscotti. They taste especially good when spread with a chocolate glaze.

3 tablespoons butter or margarine, softened
¼ cup white sugar
¼ cup firmly packed brown sugar
2 eggs
1 teaspoon vanilla extract
2 cups all-purpose flour
1½ teaspoons baking powder
½ teaspoon baking soda
¾ cup coarsely chopped pecans
Chocolate Coating (page 120) (optional)

Preheat the oven to 400° F. Grease a 10-inch by 15-inch baking sheet.

Beat together the butter or margarine and sugars until fluffy. Add the eggs and vanilla and beat until smooth.

Combine the flour, baking powder, baking soda, and pecans. Add to the egg mixture, mixing well. The dough will be stiff, but sticky.

On a floured board, divide the dough in half. Form each half into a 12-inch loaf. Pat the loaves to a diameter of 2½ inches. Place the loaves 3 inches apart on the prepared baking sheet. Bake for 20 minutes, or until firm and lightly browned. Remove from the oven and place the baking sheet on a wire rack to cool slightly. Reduce the oven temperature to 325°.

Yield: 24 biscotti

While they are still warm, slice the loaves on the diagonal into ½-inch slices. Lay cut-side down on the baking sheet. Bake for 15 minutes more, until dry and lightly browned. Place the baking sheet on a wire rack and allow the biscotti to cool completely. Then spread one side with the Chocolate Coating, if desired.

Walnut Biscotti

These biscotti are very sweet and especially crispy with lots of walnut flavor. It is possible to substitute regular vegetable oil for the walnut oil, but the taste will be slightly muted. Walnut oil is available in most gourmet food shops.

3 tablespoons walnut oil
2 eggs
½ cup white sugar
1 cup firmly packed brown sugar
2 cups all-purpose flour
1 teaspoon baking powder
½ teaspoon cinnamon
1 cup finely ground walnuts

Preheat the oven to 375° F. Grease a 10-inch by 15-inch baking sheet.

Beat together the oil and eggs until frothy. Add the sugars and continue beating until well mixed.

Combine the flour, baking powder, and cinnamon. Gradually add to the egg mixture, mixing well. Fold in the walnuts. The dough will be stiff, but sticky.

With floured hands, divide the dough in half. Shape each half into a loaf approximately 12 inches long. Place on the prepared baking sheet at least 3 inches apart. Flatten the loaves slightly. Bake for 25 minutes. Remove from the oven, place the baking sheet on a wire rack, and allow to cool slightly.

While they are still warm, slice the loaves

Yield: 48 biscotti

on the diagonal into ½-inch slices. Arrange the slices cut-side down on the baking sheet. Return to the oven and bake for an additional 20 minutes, flipping the biscotti halfway through the baking time. Place the baking sheet on a wire rack and allow the biscotti to cool completely.

Lemon-Walnut Biscotti

With some stewed fruit, these tart, crunchy biscotti make a wonderfully light finish to a pasta dinner.

3 tablespoons butter or margarine,
  melted
¼ cup white sugar
¼ cup firmly packed brown sugar
2 eggs
1 teaspoon vanilla extract
Grated rind of 1 lemon
2 tablespoons fresh lemon juice
2 cups all-purpose flour
1½ teaspoons baking powder
½ teaspoon baking soda
1 cup coarsely chopped walnuts

Yield: 48 biscotti

Preheat the oven to 400° F. Grease a 10-inch by 15-inch baking sheet.

Beat together the melted butter or margarine, sugars, and eggs, mixing well. Add the vanilla, lemon rind, and lemon juice.

Combine the flour, baking powder, baking soda, and walnuts. Add to the egg mixture, mixing well. The dough will be stiff, but sticky.

With floured hands, divide the dough in half on the baking sheet. Pat each half into a loaf 12 inches long. Space the loaves at least 3 inches apart. Flatten slightly. Bake for 20 minutes, until firm and lightly browned. Remove from the oven and place the baking sheet on a wire rack to cool slightly. Reduce the oven temperature to 325°.

While they are still slightly warm, slice the

loaves on the diagonal into ½-inch slices. Arrange the slices cut-side down on the baking sheet. Return to the oven and bake for an additional 15 minutes, or until dry. Place the baking sheet on a wire rack and allow the biscotti to cool completely.

Hazelnut Biscotti Rings

Italian bakers sometimes shape biscotti into rings or "fingers." They are still baked twice—at two different oven temperatures—and the results are crispy.

3 tablespoons hazelnut oil (available in gourmet shops)
2 eggs
1 cup sugar
2 cups all-purpose flour
1 teaspoon baking powder
½ teaspoon cinnamon
1 cup finely ground hazelnuts
1 egg white beaten with 1 tablespoon water

Preheat the oven to 350° F. Grease two 10-inch by 15-inch baking sheets.

Beat together the hazelnut oil and eggs. Gradually add the sugar, beating well.

Combine the flour, baking powder, cinnamon, and ⅔ cup of the ground hazelnuts. Add to the egg mixture, beating until a smooth, stiff dough forms.

Divide the dough into 25 pieces. Roll each piece into a 5-inch rope, then form the ropes into rings. Pinch the ends together firmly.

Place the rings 2 inches apart on the prepared baking sheets. Brush the rings with the beaten egg white mixture and sprinkle with the remaining ⅓ cup ground hazelnuts. Bake for 20 minutes. Without removing the rings from the oven, reduce the oven temperature

Yield: 25 biscotti

to 300 degrees and bake for an additional 15 minutes.

Remove from the oven and carefully transfer the rings onto wire racks. Cool completely.

Ginger Biscotti

An extra crisp version of a gingersnap, these are especially good when dipped—just long enough to soften slightly—into a steaming cup of rich cocoa.

½ cup butter or margarine, softened
¾ cup sugar
½ cup unsulphured molasses
3 eggs
3 cups all-purpose flour
1½ teaspoons baking powder
2 tablespoons ground ginger
1 tablespoon cinnamon
1 teaspoon ground nutmeg
½ teaspoon ground cloves
½ cup coarsely chopped almonds

Yield: 48 biscotti

Preheat the oven to 350° F. Grease two 10-inch by 15-inch baking sheets.

In large bowl, beat together the butter or margarine, sugar, and molasses until smooth. Add the eggs, one at a time, beating well after each addition.

Combine the flour, baking powder, spices, and almonds. Add to the egg mixture, mixing well. The dough will be stiff, but sticky.

Using floured hands, divide the dough into 4 portions. Pat each portion into a slightly flattened loaf measuring about 2 inches wide and 12 inches long. Place 2 loaves on each baking sheet, spaced evenly apart. Bake for 25 minutes, or until the loaves are browned at the edges. Remove from the oven and place the baking sheets on wire racks to cool slightly.

While they are still warm, slice the loaves on the diagonal into ½-inch slices. Arrange the slices cut-side down on the baking sheets. Return to the oven and bake for an additional 15 minutes, or until the biscotti are brown. Place the baking sheets on wire racks and allow the biscotti to cool completely.

Orange Biscotti

½ cup butter or margarine, softened
1¼ cups sugar
2 eggs
2 tablespoons grated orange rind
1 tablespoon frozen orange juice
concentrate
1 teaspoon vanilla extract
2½ cups all-purpose flour
2½ teaspoons baking powder
½ teaspoon ground ginger
½ teaspoon salt

Preheat the oven to 375° F. Grease a 10-inch by 15-inch baking sheet.

Beat together the butter or margarine and sugar until fluffy. Add the eggs, orange rind, orange juice concentrate, and vanilla, mixing well.

Combine the flour, baking powder, ginger, and salt. Add to the egg mixture, mixing well. The dough will be stiff, but sticky.

With floured hands, divide the dough in half. On the prepared baking sheet, pat each half into a loaf the length of the baking sheet. Space the loaves evenly apart on the sheet. Flatten the loaves slightly. Bake for about 20 minutes, or until lightly browned. Remove from the oven and place the baking sheet on a wire rack to cool slightly. Reduce the oven temperature to 325°.

Yield: 24 biscotti

While they are still warm, slice the loaves on the diagonal into ¾-inch slices. Arrange the slices on the baking sheet cut-side down. Return to the oven and bake for an additional 15 minutes, gently flipping the cookies halfway through the baking time. Place the baking sheet on a wire rack and allow the biscotti to cool completely.

Chocolate Biscotti

*These biscotti are not as sweet as most choco-
late cookies. They taste divine with a cup of
Amaretto-spiked hot cocoa.*

**3 tablespoons butter or margarine,
  softened**
⅔ cup sugar
2 eggs
½ teaspoon almond extract
1½ cups all-purpose flour
½ cup unsweetened cocoa powder
1½ teaspoons baking powder
½ teaspoon baking soda
**½ cup coarsely chopped almonds
  (optional)**

Preheat the oven to 350° F. Grease a 10-inch
by 15-inch baking sheet.

Beat together the butter or margarine, sugar,
eggs, and almond extract.

Combine the flour, cocoa powder, baking powder, baking soda, and almonds (if desired). Add
to the egg mixture, mixing well.

Using floured hands, divide the dough in half.
On the baking sheet, form each half into a 12-
inch loaf. Space the loaves 3 inches apart. Flatten
the loaves slightly. Bake for 25 minutes, or until
the loaves are firm when touched lightly in the
center. Remove from the oven and place the
baking sheet on a wire rack to cool slightly.

While they are still warm, slice the loaves
into ½-inch slices. Arrange the slices cut-side
down on the baking sheet. Return to the oven

Yield: 48 biscotti

and bake for an additional 20 minutes, or until the biscotti are dry and crisp. Place the baking sheet on a wire rack and allow the biscotti to cool completely.

Cinnamon Biscotti Fingers

You can count on a spicy-sweet aroma wafting through the kitchen while these biscotti are in the oven. This is an old family recipe, given to me by a friend.

3 cups all-purpose flour
½ cup sugar
2 teaspoons baking powder
1½ teaspoons cinnamon
¼ teaspoon salt
½ cup butter or margarine, chilled
2 eggs, slightly beaten
½ cup milk
½ cup finely chopped walnuts

Preheat the oven to 350° F.

In a large bowl, combine the flour, sugar, baking powder, cinnamon, and salt. With a pastry blender or your hands, work in the butter or margarine until the mixture resembles coarse crumbs. Mix in the eggs and milk until the dough forms a ball. Knead the dough until it is smooth and stiff.

Divide the dough into 40 pieces. Roll each piece into a 3-inch rope. Place the ropes 1 inch apart on an ungreased 10-inch by 15-inch baking sheet. Sprinkle with the chopped walnuts. Bake for 15 minutes.

Reduce the oven temperature to 300° (do not remove biscotti from the oven). Bake for an additional 10 minutes, or until the biscotti are golden brown. Place the baking sheet on a wire rack and allow the biscotti to cool completely.

Yield: 40 biscotti

Almond Biscotti

These biscotti are for serious almond lovers.

**2 tablespoons butter or margarine,
     softened**
¾ cup sugar
2 eggs
2 teaspoons almond extract
2¼ cups all-purpose flour
1½ teaspoons baking powder
¼ teaspoon salt
⅔ cup finely ground almonds
1 egg white, slightly beaten

Preheat the oven to 400° F. Grease a 10-inch by 15-inch baking sheet.

Beat together the butter or margarine, sugar, whole eggs, and almond extract until smooth.

Combine the flour, baking powder, salt, and almonds. Add to egg mixture, mixing into a smooth, stiff dough.

Divide the dough into 4 equal portions. On the baking sheet, form each portion of dough into a cigar-shaped loaf and space the loaves evenly apart. Brush the egg white on each of the loaves. Bake for 20 minutes or until lightly brown. Remove from the oven and place the baking sheet on a wire rack to cool for 5 minutes.

Slice loaves diagonally into 1-inch slices. Arrange cut-side down on the baking sheet and bake 5 minutes, or until crisp. Place the sheet on a wire rack and allow to cool completely.

Yield: 20 biscotti

Red Wine Biscotti

These sweet, wine-flavored biscuits are delicious dipped in red wine or coffee. Any full-bodied red wine can be used, but remember: The better the wine, the better the cookie.

1 cup vegetable oil
1 egg
⅔ cup sugar
5 cups all-purpose flour
2 teaspoons baking powder
½ teaspoon salt
1 cup red wine (a Merlot or Cabernet is
  especially delicious)

Preheat the oven to 375° F. Grease two 10-inch by 15-inch baking sheets.

Beat together the oil and egg until frothy. Add the sugar and continue beating until well mixed.

In a separate bowl, combine the flour, baking powder, and salt. Gradually add to the egg mixture alternately with the red wine. Mix until a smooth dough forms. The dough will be stiff, but sticky.

With floured hands, divide the dough in half. Form each half into a 12-inch loaf and place on the prepared baking sheets. Flatten the loaves to a 4-inch width. Bake for 25 minutes or until the loaves are lightly browned and firm to the touch. Remove from the oven and place the baking sheets on wire racks to cool slightly. Reduce the oven temperature to 350°.

Yield: 48 biscotti

While they are still warm, slice the loaves on the diagonal into ½-inch slices. Arrange the slices cut-side down on the baking sheets. Return to the oven and bake for an additional 20 minutes, or until the biscotti are dry and crisp. Place the baking sheets on wire racks and allow the biscotti to cool completely.

Apricot Biscotti

The goodness of whole wheat flour and the tartness of dried apricots combine to make this one of my favorite biscotti.

½ cup vegetable oil
1 cup white sugar
½ cup firmly packed brown sugar
2 eggs
¼ cup brandy
2½ cups all-purpose flour
1 cup whole wheat flour
1½ teaspoons baking powder
¼ teaspoon salt
1 cup finely ground pecans
1 cup finely diced dried apricots

Yield: 30 biscotti

Preheat the oven to 375° F. Grease two 10-inch by 15-inch baking sheets.

Beat together the oil, sugars, and eggs until frothy. Add the brandy, mixing well.

Combine the flours, baking powder, salt, and pecans. Add to the egg mixture, mixing well. Fold in the dried apricots. The dough will be very stiff.

With floured hands, divide the dough in half. Form each half into a loaf 10 inches long and approximately 4 inches wide. Place a loaf on each prepared baking sheet and flatten slightly. Bake for 25 minutes, or until the loaves are firm to the touch and lightly brown. Remove from the oven and place the baking sheets on wire racks to cool for 10 minutes.

Slice the loaves into ¾-inch slices. Arrange

cut-side down on the baking sheets. Return to the oven and bake for 20 minutes, or until dry and crisp. Place the baking sheets on wire racks and allow the biscotti to cool completely.

Anise Slices

Recipes for anise-flavored biscotti appear quite often in Italian cookbooks. This version uses the aromatic licorice-flavored seeds and couples it with a pleasant lemon flavor. The variation given below uses anise extract.

⅔ cup vegetable oil
1 cup sugar
3 eggs
1 tablespoon grated lemon rind
½ teaspoon lemon extract
3 cups all-purpose flour
2½ teaspoons baking powder
2 teaspoons ground anise seed
⅛ teaspoon salt

Preheat the oven to 375° F. Grease a 10-inch by 15-inch baking sheet.

Beat together the oil, sugar, and eggs until frothy. Add the lemon rind and lemon extract, mixing well.

Combine the flour, baking powder, ground anise seed, and salt. Gradually add to the egg mixture, beating until a stiff dough forms.

With floured hands, divide the dough in half. Shape each half into a thin loaf, approximately 14 inches long, with a diameter of 2 inches. Place the loaves at least 4 inches apart on the prepared baking sheet. Flatten the loaves slightly. Bake for 25 minutes, or until the loaves are lightly browned. Remove from the oven and place the baking sheet on a wire rack to cool for 15 minutes.

Yield: 40 biscotti

Slice the loaves on the diagonal into ½-inch slices. Arrange cut-side down on the baking sheet. Return to the oven and bake for an additional 15 minutes, flipping the slices halfway through the baking time. Place the baking sheet on a wire rack and allow the biscotti to cool completely.

Anise Slices II

Substitute 1 teaspoon anise extract for the ground anise seed and add with the lemon extract.

Mandelbread

Mandelbread, or mandelbrot, is the northern European version of biscotti. This particular cookie has the subtle tang of citrus in addition to the crunch of almonds.

¼ cup vegetable oil
1 cup sugar
3 eggs
3 tablespoons lemon juice
¼ cup orange juice
2 teaspoons grated lemon rind
2 teaspoons grated orange rind
2½ cups all-purpose flour
1 teaspoon baking powder
½ teaspoon cinnamon
¼ teaspoon salt
1 cup chopped almonds

Yield: 30 cookies

Preheat the oven to 350° F. Grease a 10-inch by 15-inch baking sheet.

Beat together the oil, sugar, and eggs until light and frothy. Add the lemon juice, orange juice, and grated rinds, mixing well.

Combine the flour, baking powder, cinnamon, salt, and almonds. Gradually add to the egg mixture, beating until a soft dough forms. The dough will be sticky, but stiff.

With floured hands, divide the dough in half. Form each half into a loaf and place the loaves 3 inches apart on the prepared baking sheet. Flatten slightly. Bake for 30 minutes. Remove from the oven and place the baking sheet on a wire rack to cool slightly.

While they are still warm, slice the loaves on the diagonal into ½-inch slices. Arrange

cut-side down on the baking sheet. Bake for an additional 15 minutes. Place the baking sheet on a wire rack and allow the mandel-bread to cool completely

Cinnamon Mandelbread

Sprinkle the slices liberally with a mixture of ¼ cup sugar and 2 tablespoons cinnamon just before the second baking.

Berti's Mandelbread

Berti Aronow, the mother of my good friend, Denise Aronow, contributed this recipe. Her version calls for nutmeg instead of the usual cinnamon, which results in a spicy, yet not overly sweet cookie.

4 eggs, at room temperature
1 cup sugar
½ teaspoon ground nutmeg
¾ cup vegetable oil
1 teaspoon vanilla extract
3¾ cups all-purpose flour
2 teaspoons baking powder
¼ teaspoon salt
½ cup coarsely chopped blanched
**   almonds**

Yield: 30 to 40 cookies

Preheat the oven to 350° F. Grease two 10-inch by 15-inch baking sheets.

Beat together the eggs, sugar, and nutmeg until frothy. Slowly beat in the oil, mixing well. Add the vanilla.

Combine the flour, baking powder, and salt. Add to the egg mixture, beating until a soft dough forms. Fold in the almonds.

On a lightly floured board, shape the dough into four 10-inch loaves. Arrange 2 on each prepared baking sheet, spacing them 3 inches apart. Bake for 20 minutes, or until firm to the touch and very lightly browned. Remove from oven and place the baking sheets on wire racks to cool for 5 minutes.

While they are still warm, slice the loaves on the diagonal into ½-inch slices. Arrange cut-

side down on the baking sheets. Bake for an additional 10 to 15 minutes, until crisp and golden brown. Place the baking sheets on wire racks and allow the mandelbread to cool completely.

Chocolate Coating

This coating is especially recommended for the Basic Biscotti because it hardens nicely and doesn't require refrigeration. Experiment with this glaze on any other flavored biscotti—you might discover a delicious new flavor combination.

2 tablespoons vegetable oil
1 cup semi-sweet chocolate chips

In a small saucepan, heat the oil over medium-high heat until you can see the oil swirl (about 160° on a candy thermometer). Add the chocolate chips to the oil and heat, stirring constantly, until the temperature reaches 150°, about 1 minute. Remove from the heat and let cool slightly. Spread on top or dip each biscotti in the chocolate.

Index

A

Almond(s). *See also* Brownies; Nut bars
  Bars, 80
  Biscotti, 109
  Shortbread, 53
  White Chocolate Brownies, 42
Anise Slices, 114–115
Apple(s). *See also* Applesauce Brownies
  Bars, Yogurt, 72
  Butter Bars, Layered, 81
  -Cheese Pleasers, 71
  Coconut Bars, Crunchy, 82–83
  Pecan Squares, 70
Applesauce Brownies, 34
Apricot(s)
  Bars, 73
  Biscotti, 112–113
  -Granola Treats, 65

B

Baking chocolate, 10
Baking tips, brownies, 8–9
Banana Granola Bars, 66
Basic Biscotti, 94–95
Berti's Mandelbread, 118–119
Biscotti
  Almond, 109
  Anise Slices, 114–115
  Apricot, 112–113
  Basic, 94–95
  Chocolate, 106–107
  Fingers, Cinnamon, 108
  Ginger, 102–103
  Lemon-Walnut, 98–99
  Mandelbread, 116–117
  Berti's, 118–119
  Cinnamon, 117

Orange, 104–105
Red Wine, 110–111
Rings, Hazelnut, 100–101
storage of, 93
Walnut, 96–97
Blarney Stones, 58–59
Blondies, 56
Brownie(s)
Almond White Chocolate, 42
Applesauce, 34
baking tips, 8–9
Buttermilk, 32–33
Cherry Oat, 36
Chewy White Chocolate, 24
Chocolate Crunch, 43
Chocolate Syrup, 31
Classic Cake, 30
Classic Fudge, 12
Coconut Fudge Dreams, 37
Cream Cheese, 40–41
Crème de Cacao, 15
Double Chocolate, 14
Double Chocolate Fruit, 14
food processors and, 8–9

freezing, 9
Frosted Fudge, 13
Fruit Bars, 18
Quick, 18–19
Fruited, 17
Grand Marnier, 15
Hawaiian, 38-39
Honey Pecan, 20–21
Layered Oat, 29
Layered Peppermint, 26–27
Macaroon, 28
Mae's Triple Chocolate Quick, 45
Marbled, 25
Milk Chocolate, 23
Quick Turtle, 44
Raisin Fudge, 22
Raspberry, 16
Rolo, 35
Torte
Chocolate, 46–47
Coffee, 50
Sweetheart, 48–49
Buttermilk Brownies, 32–33
Butterscotch Bars, 57

C

Cake brownies, 30-44
  baking tip, 9
  Classic, 30
Candy
  Quick Turtle Brownies, 44
  Rolo Brownies, 35
Caramel Granola Bars, 67
Carrot Bars, Oatmeal, 63
Cheese Pleasers, Apple-, 71
Cheesecake Squares, 79
Cherry Bars, Old-Fashioned, 84
Cherry Oat Brownies, 36
Cherry Squares, 74
Chewy White Chocolate Brownies, 24
Chocolate, 9–11. *See also* Brownies
  baking tips, 8–9
  Biscotti, 106–107
  Blondies, 56
  Brownie Torte, 46–47
  Cherry Squares, 74
  Coating, 120
  Crunch Brownies, 43
  Glaze, 36, 48–49
  Peanut Butter Marble Bars, 61

  Syrup Brownies, 31
Cinnamon Biscotti Fingers, 108
Cinnamon Mandelbread, 117
Classic Cake Brownies, 30
Classic Fudge Brownies, 12
Cocoa powder, 10–11
Cocoa-Nut Icing, 32–33
Coconut
  Banana Granola Bars, 66
  Bars, Crunchy Apple, 82–83
  Cookie Bars, 78
  Fudge Dreams, 37
  Granola Bars, 64
  Macadamia Nut Bars, 86
  Macaroon Brownies, 28
  Peanut Butter Oat Squares, 62
Coffee
  Bars, 55
  Brownie Torte, 50
  Frosting, 50
Cranberry-Prune Squares, 75
Cream Cheese Brownies, 40–41
Crème de Cacao Brownies, 15
Crunchy Apple Coconut Bars, 82–83

D

Date Bars, 76
Double Chocolate Brownies, 14
Double Chocolate Fruit Brownies, 14

F

Food processors, brownies made in, 8–9
Freezing
  brownies, 9
  fruit and nut bars, 52
Frosted Fudge Brownies, 13
Frosting. *See also* Glaze, Icing
  Coffee, 50
  Fudge, 13
Fruit bars
  Apple Pecan Squares, 70
  Apple-Cheese Pleasers, 71
  Apricot Bars, 73
  Apricot-Granola Treats, 65
  Banana Granola Bars, 66
  Brownies, 18
  Cherry Squares, 74
  Cranberry-Prune Squares, 75
  Crunchy Apple Coconut Bars, 82–83
  Date Bars, 76

  freezing, 52
  Granola Bars, 64
  Layered Apple Butter Bars, 81
  Lemon Bars, 85
  Oatmeal Carrot Bars, 63
  Old-Fashioned Cherry Bars, 84
  Persimmon Spice Squares, 77
  Pumpkin Pie Squares, 88–89
  Quick Brownie, 18-19
  Raisin Bran Spice Bars, 69
  Raisin Oat Squares, 68
  Whole Grain Jam Squares, 90
  Yogurt Apple Bars, 72
Fruited Brownies, 17
Fudge brownies, 12–29
  baking tip, 9
  Classic, 12
  Frosted, 13
  Raisin, 22
Fudge Frosting, 13

G

Ginger Biscotti, 102–103
Glaze, Chocolate, 36, 48–49, 120. *See also*
  Frosting; Icing

Grand Marnier Brownies, 15
Granola Bars, 64
  Apricot-, Treats, 65
  Banana, 66
  Caramel, 67

H

Hawaiian Brownies, 38-39
Hazelnut Biscotti Rings, 100–101
Honey
  Icing, 20–21
  Pecan Brownies, 20–21

I

Icing. *See also* Frosting; Glaze
  Cocoa-Nut, 32–33
  Honey, 20–21
  Vanilla, 38-39

J

Jam Squares, Whole Grain, 90

L

Layered Apple Butter Bars, 81

Layered Oat Brownies, 29
Layered Peppermint Brownies, 26–27
Lemon Bars, 85
Lemon-Walnut Biscotti, 98–99

M

Macadamia Nut Bars, 86
Macaroon Brownies, 28
Mae's Triple Chocolate Quick Brownies, 45
Mandelbread, 116–117
  Berti's, 117–118
  Cinnamon, 116
Marbled Brownies, 25
Marshmallow, Chocolate Crunch Brownies, 43
Microwaves, melting chocolate in, 8
Milk chocolate, 10
  Brownies, 23

N

Nut bars. *See also* Brownies
  Almond Bars, 80
  Almond Shortbread, 53
  Apple Pecan Squares, 70
  Blarney Stones, 58–59
  Blondies, 56

Butterscotch Bars, 57
Caramel Granola Bars, 67
Cheesecake Squares, 79
Cherry Squares, 74
Coconut Cookie Bars, 78
Coffee Bars, 55
Cranberry-Prune Squares, 75
Date Bars, 76
freezing, 52
Granola Bars, 64
Layered Apple Butter Bars, 81
Macadamia, 86
Peanut Butter
Marble Bars, 61
Oat Squares, 62
Squares, 60
Pecan Bars, 54
Pecan Cookie Bars, 87
Persimmon Spice Squares, 77
Raisin Bran Spice Bars, 69
Raisin Oat Squares, 68
Whole Grain Jam Squares, 90

O

Oat Brownies

Cherry, 36
Layered, 29
Oat Squares
Peanut Butter, 62
Raisin, 68
Oatmeal Carrot Bars, 63
Old-Fashioned Cherry Bars, 84
Orange Biscotti, 104–105

P

Peanut Butter
Chocolate Crunch Brownies, 43
Marble Bars, 61
Oat Squares, 62
Squares, 60
Pecan. *See also* Nut bars
Bars, 54
Brownies, Honey, 22
Cookie Bars, 87
Peppermint Brownies, Layered, 26–27
Persimmon Spice Squares, 77
Pineapple, Hawaiian Brownies, 38-39
Prune Squares, Cranberry-, 75
Pumpkin Pie Squares, 88–89

Q

Quick Brownie Fruit Bars, 18–19
Quick Turtle Brownies, 44

R

Raisin
  Bran Spice Bars, 69
  Fudge Brownies, 22
  Oat Squares, 68
Raspberry Brownies, 16
Red Wine Biscotti, 110–111
Rolo Brownies, 35

S

Semi-sweet chocolate, 10
Storing biscotti, 93
Sweetheart Brownie Torte, 48–49

T

Torte
  Chocolate Brownie, 46–47
  Coffee Brownie, 50

Sweetheart Brownie, 48–49
Triple Chocolate Quick Brownies, Mae's, 45

U

Unsweetened baking chocolate, 10
Unsweetened cocoa powder, 10–11

V

Vanilla Icing, 38-39

W

Walnut. *See also* Brownies; Nut bars
  Biscotti, 96–97
  Lemon-, 98–99
White chocolate, 11
  Brownies
  Almond, 42
  Chewy, 24
Whole Grain Jam Squares, 90

Y

Yogurt Apple Bars, 72

OTHER SPECIALTY COOKBOOKS FROM THE CROSSING PRESS

SAUCES FOR PASTA! By Kristie Trabant	$8.95	**LOW CHOLESTEROL DESSERTS!** By Terri Siegel	$8.95
PESTOS! By Dorothy Rankin	$8.95	**SALSAS!** By Andrea Chesman	$8.95
PASTA SALADS! By Susan Janine Meyer	$8.95	**GOOD FOR YOU COOKIES!** By Jane Marsh Dieckmann	$8.95
SALAD DRESSINGS! By Jane Marsh Dieckmann	$8.95	**OLD WORLD BREADS!** By Charel Scheele	$8.95
FRUIT DESSERTS! By Dorothy Parker	$8.95	**SORBETS!** By Jim Tarantino	$8.95
FAST BREADS! By Howard Early and Glenda Morris	$8.95	**SUN-DRIED TOMATOES!** By Andrea Chesman	$8.95
CONDIMENTS! By Jay Solomon	$8.95	**SPOON DESSERTS!** By Lynn Nusom	$8.95

Available at your local bookstore, or write directly to The Crossing Press, P. O. Box 1048, Freedom, CA 95019. Please add $2.00 for postage on the first book, and $ .50 for each additional book. If you wish, you may use VISA or MASTERCARD. Call 800/777-1048 to place your order. Please give your number and expiration date.

We publish many more cookbooks. Call 800/777-1048 to request a free catalog.